First World War
and Army of Occupation
War Diary
France, Belgium and Germany

42 DIVISION
Divisional Troops
Royal Army Veterinary Corps
19 Mobile Veterinary Section
1 March 1917 - 31 March 1919

WO95/2653/1

The Naval & Military Press Ltd
www.nmarchive.com
Published in association with The National Archives

Published by

The Naval & Military Press Ltd

Unit 10 Ridgewood Industrial Park,

Uckfield, East Sussex,

TN22 5QE England

Tel: +44 (0) 1825 749494

www.naval-military-press.com

www.nmarchive.com

This diary has been reprinted in facsimile from the original. Any imperfections are inevitably reproduced and the quality may fall short of modern type and cartographic standards.

© Crown Copyright
Images reproduced by permission of The National Archives, London, England, 2015.

Contents

Document type	Place/Title	Date From	Date To
Heading	WO95/2653/1 1 19 Mobile Vet Section Mar'17-Mar'19		
Heading	42nd Division 19th Mobile Vety Secn. Mar 1917-Mar 1919		
Heading	War Diary O.C. 19"Mobile Veterinary Section For The Month Of March 1917 Vol. III		
Miscellaneous	A.D.V.S. 42nd Division.	04/04/1917	04/04/1917
War Diary	Marseilles	01/03/1917	03/03/1917
War Diary	Pont Remy	04/03/1917	04/03/1917
War Diary	Hallencourt	04/03/1917	30/03/1917
War Diary	St. Saveur	31/03/1917	31/03/1917
War Diary	Hamel	31/03/1917	31/03/1917
Heading	War Diary for the Month Of April 1917 O.C. 19th Mobile Veterinary Section Vol.IV		
War Diary	Hamel Mericourt	01/04/1917	22/04/1917
War Diary	Halle	22/04/1917	30/04/1917
Heading	War Diary for the Month Of May 1917 O.C. 19th Mobile Veterinary Section		
War Diary	Halle	01/05/1917	02/05/1917
War Diary	Buire	03/05/1917	08/05/1917
War Diary	Marquaix	09/05/1917	20/05/1917
War Diary	Rocquigny	21/05/1917	31/05/1917
Heading	War Diary for the Month Of June 1917 O.C. 19th Mobile Veterinary Section. Vol VI		
War Diary	Rocquigny	01/06/1917	30/06/1917
Heading	War Diary For Month Of July 1917 OC 19th Mobile Veterinary Section Vol 6		
War Diary	Rocquigny	01/07/1917	08/07/1917
War Diary	Achietc Pent	09/07/1917	31/07/1917
Heading	War Diary Month August 1917 OC 19 Mobile Veterinary Section. Vol 7		
War Diary	Achiet & Petit	01/08/1917	21/08/1917
War Diary	Aveluy	22/08/1917	22/08/1917
War Diary	Albert	23/08/1917	23/08/1917
War Diary	Godewaersvelde	23/08/1917	23/08/1917
War Diary	Watou	24/08/1917	30/08/1917
War Diary	Map Sheet 28 C 14. 6.5.4	31/08/1917	31/08/1917
Heading	War Diary for the Month Ending September 1917 O.C. 19th Mobile Veterinary Section. Vol IX		
War Diary	Poperinghe	01/09/1917	19/09/1917
War Diary	Winnezeele	19/09/1917	21/09/1917
War Diary	Woltmhoudt	22/09/1917	22/09/1917
War Diary	La Panne	23/09/1917	25/09/1917
War Diary	Coxyde Bains	26/09/1917	28/09/1917
War Diary	Saint Idesbald	29/09/1917	30/09/1917
Heading	War Diary for the Month ending October 1917 OC 19th Mobile Veterinary Section Vol VII		
War Diary	St. Idesbald	01/10/1917	06/10/1917
War Diary	Sheet 27 W.18 C. 5.7	07/10/1917	31/10/1917
Heading	War Diary for the Month Of November 1917 O.C. 19th Mobile Veterinary Section Vol 10		

War Diary	Coxyde	01/11/1917	21/11/1917
War Diary	Ghyvelde	22/11/1917	22/11/1917
War Diary	Wormhoudt	23/11/1917	23/11/1917
War Diary	Zermezeele	24/11/1917	24/11/1917
War Diary	Houdegham	25/11/1917	25/11/1917
War Diary	Lambres	26/11/1917	28/11/1917
War Diary	Essars	29/11/1917	30/11/1917
War Diary	Coxyde	01/11/1917	21/11/1917
War Diary	Ghyvelde	22/11/1917	22/11/1917
War Diary	Wormhoudt	23/11/1917	23/11/1917
War Diary	Zermezeele	24/11/1917	24/11/1917
War Diary	Houdegham	25/11/1917	25/11/1917
War Diary	Lambres	26/11/1917	28/11/1917
War Diary	Essars	29/11/1917	30/11/1917
Heading	War Diary for The Month ending December 1917 O.C. 19th Mobile Veterinary Section Vol II		
War Diary	Essars	01/12/1917	31/12/1917
Heading	War Diary for the month of January 1918 O.C. 19th Mobile Veterinary Section Vol 12		
War Diary	Essars	01/01/1918	31/01/1918
Heading	War Diary for the Month Of February 1918 O.C. 19th Mobile Veterinary Section. Vol 13		
War Diary	Essars	01/02/1918	16/02/1918
War Diary	Hesdigneul	17/02/1918	28/02/1918
War Diary	Essars	01/02/1918	15/02/1918
War Diary	Hesdigneul	17/02/1918	28/02/1918
War Diary	War Diary for the Month ending March 1918. O.C. 19th Mobile Veterinary Section. Vol 14		
War Diary	Hesdigneul	01/03/1918	23/03/1918
War Diary	Tincques	23/03/1918	24/03/1918
War Diary	Abllinzeville	25/03/1918	25/03/1918
War Diary	Bein-Villers	26/03/1918	26/03/1918
War Diary	St Rmand	26/03/1918	28/03/1918
War Diary	Hesdigneul	01/03/1918	23/03/1918
War Diary	Tincques	24/03/1918	24/03/1918
War Diary	Ablainzeville	25/03/1918	25/03/1918
War Diary	Bein-Villers	26/03/1918	26/03/1918
War Diary	St Amand	26/03/1918	28/03/1918
War Diary	Couin	29/03/1918	31/03/1918
Heading	War Diary for the month ending April 1918 O.C. 19th Mobile Veterinary Section. Vol 15		
War Diary	Couin	01/04/1918	02/04/1918
War Diary	Souastre	03/04/1918	07/04/1918
War Diary	Pas	08/04/1918	14/04/1918
War Diary	Bois de St Pierre	15/04/1918	30/04/1918
War Diary	Couin	01/04/1918	02/04/1918
War Diary	Souastre	03/04/1918	07/04/1918
War Diary	Pas	08/04/1918	14/04/1918
War Diary	Bois de St Pierre	15/04/1918	30/04/1918
War Diary	War Diary for the month ending May 1918. O.C. 19th Mobile Veterinary Section. Vol 16		
War Diary	Bois De St Pierre	01/05/1918	31/05/1918
Miscellaneous	Q 1/e AVC Base Records.	01/08/1918	01/08/1918
War Diary	Bois De St. Pierre	01/05/1918	31/05/1918
Heading	War Diary for the month ending June 1918. O.C. 19th Mobile Veterinary Section. Vol 17		

War Diary	Bois De. St Pierre	01/06/1918	07/06/1918
War Diary	Louvencourt	08/06/1918	30/06/1918
War Diary	Bois De. St Pierre	01/06/1918	07/06/1918
War Diary	Louvencourt	08/06/1918	30/06/1918
Heading	War Diary for the month ending July 1918 O.C. 19th Mobile Veterinary Section. Vol 18		
Miscellaneous	Q 1/e. A.V.C. Records.	13/11/1918	13/11/1918
War Diary	Louvencourt	01/07/1918	31/07/1918
Heading	War Diary for the month ending August 1918 O.C. 19th Mobile Veterinary Section Vol 19		
War Diary	Louvencourt	01/08/1918	25/08/1918
War Diary	Bertrancourt	26/08/1918	27/08/1918
War Diary	Colincamps	28/08/1918	30/08/1918
War Diary	Mibaumont	31/08/1918	31/08/1918
War Diary	Louvencourt	01/08/1918	25/08/1918
War Diary	Bertrancourt	26/08/1918	27/08/1918
War Diary	Colincamps	28/08/1918	30/08/1918
War Diary	Miraumont	31/08/1918	31/08/1918
Heading	War Diary for the month ending Sept 1918 OC. 19th Mobile Veterinary Section Vol 20		
Miscellaneous	Officer i/c R.A.V.C Records.	31/12/1918	31/12/1918
War Diary	Miraumont	01/09/1918	04/09/1918
War Diary	Warlencourt Eaucourt	05/09/1918	21/09/1918
War Diary	Fremicourt	22/09/1918	27/09/1918
War Diary	Lebucquiere	28/09/1918	30/09/1918
War Diary	Royaulcourt	30/09/1918	30/09/1918
War Diary	Miraumont	01/09/1918	04/09/1918
War Diary	Warlencourt Eaucourt	05/09/1918	21/09/1918
War Diary	Fremicourt	22/09/1918	27/09/1918
War Diary	Lebucquiere	28/09/1918	30/09/1918
War Diary	Ruyaulcourt	30/09/1918	30/09/1918
Heading	War Diary for the month ending October 1918 OC 19th Mobile Veterinary Section. Vol. 23		
Miscellaneous	O i/c R.A.V.C Records.	05/02/1919	05/02/1919
War Diary	Ruyaulcourt	01/10/1918	08/10/1918
War Diary	Trescault	09/10/1918	10/10/1918
War Diary	Les Rues Des Vignes	11/10/1918	12/10/1918
War Diary	Esnes	13/10/1918	14/10/1918
War Diary	Beauvois	14/10/1918	31/10/1918
Heading	Duplicate Copy of War Diary for the month ending October 1918 OC 19th Mobile Veterinary Section		
War Diary	Ruyaulcourt	01/10/1918	08/10/1918
War Diary	Trescault	09/10/1918	09/10/1918
War Diary	Les Rues Des Vignes	10/10/1918	12/10/1918
War Diary	Esnes	12/10/1918	14/10/1918
War Diary	Beauvois	14/10/1918	31/10/1918
Miscellaneous	War Diary for the month ending November 1918 OC. 19th Mobile Veterinary Section. Vol 23		
War Diary	Beauvois	01/11/1918	04/11/1918
War Diary	Solesmes	04/11/1918	06/11/1918
War Diary	Le Quesnoy	07/11/1918	09/11/1918
War Diary	Hargnies	10/11/1918	30/11/1918
War Diary	Beauvois	01/11/1918	04/11/1918
War Diary	Solesmes	05/11/1918	06/11/1918
War Diary	Le Quesnoy	07/11/1918	09/11/1918
War Diary	Harghies	10/11/1918	30/11/1918

Heading	War Diary. for the month ending December 1918. O.C. 19th Mobile Veterinary Section. Vol 24		
Miscellaneous	Officer Commanding. No. 19th. M.V.S	23/04/1919	23/04/1919
Miscellaneous	D I/e RAVC Records.	16/04/1919	16/04/1919
Miscellaneous	On His Majesty's Service. The Off.		
War Diary	Hargnies	01/12/1918	14/12/1918
War Diary	Marpent	14/12/1918	15/12/1918
War Diary	Lobbes	16/12/1918	18/12/1918
War Diary	Gilly	19/12/1918	31/12/1918
War Diary	Hargnies	01/12/1918	14/12/1918
War Diary	Marpent	14/12/1918	15/12/1918
War Diary	Lobbes	15/12/1918	18/12/1918
War Diary	Gilly	19/12/1918	31/12/1918
Heading	War Diary. for the month ending January 1919 OC. 19th Mobile Veterinary Section. Vol 25		
War Diary	Gilly	01/01/1919	31/01/1919
Heading	War Diary 19th M.V.S 42 DW February 1919 Vol 26		
War Diary	Gilly	01/02/1919	28/02/1919
Heading	War Diary. 19th Mobile Vety Sec. From 1/3/19 To 31/3/19 Vol 27		
War Diary	Gilly	01/03/1919	31/03/1919

WO95/2653 (1)

19 Mobil Vet Section

Mar '17 – Mar '19

42ND DIVISION

19TH MOBILE VETY SECN.
MAR 1917-MAR 1919

Vol 2

Confidential

WAR DIARY

O.C. 19ᵗʰ MOBILE VETERINARY SECTION.

For the month of MARCH 1917

Vol. III

A.D.V.S.
42nd Division

No. 19 MOBILE VETERINARY SECTION
No. 99
Date 3/4/17

Herewith AFC 2118 for the month of March please

In the Field

A R Stkus Capt. A.V.C.
O/C 19th Mobile Vety Section

General Staff
42nd Divn

Forwarded,

Jos Gillies Major
A.D.V.S
42nd Divn

*D. OF V.S.
No.
4.4.17
DIVISION*

WAR DIARY or INTELLIGENCE SUMMARY

Army Form C. 2118.

(Erase heading not required.)

Hour, Date, Place		Summary of Events and Information	Remarks and references to Appendices
0600	1-3-17 MARSEILLES	Remained at Marseilles WPS	
0830	2-3-17 "	Left Marseilles Docks WPS	
	"	Entrained Section and Horses WPS	
1600	3-3-17	In the train nothing to report WPS	
1630	4-3-17 PONT REMY	Arrived at Pont Remy WPS	
1800	"	Detrained Section and Horses, and proceeded to Hallencourt WPS	
	" HALLENCOURT	Took over Billets for men and Horses WPS	
	5-3-17 "	Nothing to report. WPS	
	6-3-17 "	Nothing to report. WPS	
	7-3-17 "	Nothing to report. WPS	
	8-3-17 "	Supply Line Transport drawn, to complete War Establishment. WPS	
	9-3-17 "	Nothing to report. WPS	
	10-3-17 "	Nothing to report. WPS	
	11-3-17 "	One man sent to 42nd Divnl Train to be permanently attached. WPS	
	12-3-17 "	Nothing to report. WPS	
	13-3-17 "	Nothing to report. WPS	
	14-3-17 "	Nothing to report. WPS	
	15-3-17 "	Civilian riding Horses drawn from Remount Depot Abbeville, to complete War Establishment. WPS	
	16-3-17 "	Nothing to report. WPS	
	17-3-17 "	Nothing to report. WPS	
	18-3-17 "	Nothing to report. WPS	
	19-3-17 "	Two sick horses evacuated to 22nd Veterinary Hospital. WPS	
	20-3-17 "	Nothing to report. WPS	
	21-3-17 "	Nothing to report. WPS	
	22-3-17 "	Nothing to report. WPS	
	23-3-17 "	Two sick horses evacuated to 22nd Veterinary Hospital. WPS	
	24-3-17 "	Two sick horses evacuated to 22nd Veterinary Hospital. WPS	
	25-3-17 "	One R.A.O. 1st Corps transferred to No 2 Veterinary Hospital. WPS	
	26-3-17 "	One man admitted to field Ambulance. WPS Six sick horses evacuated to 22nd Veterinary Hospital. WPS

Clarke Capt R.V.C.
O.C. 19 Mobile Veterinary Section

Army Form C. 2118.

WAR DIARY
or
INTELLIGENCE SUMMARY

(Erase heading not required.)

Instructions regarding War Diaries and Intelligence Summaries are contained in F. S. Regs., Part II. and the Staff Manual respectively. Title pages will be prepared in manuscript.

Hour, Date, Place	Summary of Events and Information	Remarks and references to Appendices
27/3/17 HALLENCOURT	Two O.R. reported their arrival for duty. WS	
28/3/17 "	Five sick animals evacuated 22nd VETERINARY HOSPITAL WS	
29/3/17 "	Two sick animals evacuated 22nd VETERINARY HOSPITAL WS	
30/3/17 "	According to instructions received from 41st DIVISIONAL HQrs proceeded by route march to SAINT SAVEUR WS	
8-30pm 31/3/17 St SAVEUR	Left SAINT SAVEUR WS	
4-30pm	Arrived at HAMEL and Billeted for night WS	

CONFIDENTIAL

War Diary.

Vol 3

For the Month of APRIL 1917.

O.C. 19th Mobile Veterinary Section.

Vol. IV

WAR DIARY

Army Form C. 2118.

Instructions regarding War Diaries and Intelligence Summaries are contained in F. S. Regs., Part II. and the Staff Manual respectively. Title pages will be prepared in manuscript.

(Erase heading not required.)

Hour, Date, Place	Summary of Events and Information	Remarks and references to Appendices
9.30am 1-4-17 HAMEL	Section left HAMEL WB WB	
11.30am MERICOURT	Arrived at MERICOURT	
2-4-17	Took over Billets for men and horse WB	
3-4-17	Nothing to report WB	
4-4-17	Nothing to report WB	
5-4-17	One N.C.O. & men WB two arrived for duty from No.2 VETERINARY HOSPITAL WB	
6-4-17	Nothing to report WB	
7-4-17	One Man Leopold to Establishment returned to No.2 VETERINARY HOSPITAL WB	
8-4-17	Nothing to report WB	
9-4-17	Horse AMBULANCE received to Complete War Establishment WB	
10-4-17	One man attached to FIELD AMBULANCE WB	
11-4-17	Four sick animals evacuated to No.7 VETERINARY HOSPITAL WB	
12-4-17	Nothing to report WB	
13-4-17	Subject to report WB	
14-4-17	Nothing to report WB	
15-4-17	Fourteen Sick animals evacuated to No.7 VETERINARY HOSPITAL WB	
16-4-17	Nothing to report WB	
17-4-17	Nothing to report WB	
18-4-17	Twenty nine Sick animals evacuated to No.7 VETERINARY HOSPITAL WB	
19-4-17	Nothing to report WB	
20-4-17	One SHOEING SMITH reported for arrival for duty from No.2 VETERINARY HOSPITAL WB	
21-4-17	Nothing to report WB	
22-4-17	Received orders from A.D.V.S. H.Q. "A" Division to move Section to HALLE left WB	
	Evacuated Sixteen Sick animals to No.2 MOBILE VETERINARY SECTION WB	
10 am HALLE	Left MERICOURT WB	
2 pm "	Arrived at HALLE WB	
	Took over Billets from O.C. 1/1 MIDLAND MOBILE VETERINARY SECTION. WB	
23-4-17	One man reported his arrival from HOSPITAL WB	
24-4-17	Nothing to report WB	
25-4-17	One Man attached to WB	
26-4-17	Nothing to report WB	
27-4-17	One man Leopold Two arrived for duty from No.10 VET VETERINARY HOSPITAL WB	
28-4-17	One man Leopold to Establishment returned to No.2 VETERINARY HOSPITAL WB	
29-4-17	One A.S.C. DRIVER Horse AMBULANCE reported his arrival for duty WB	
	Thirty sick animals evacuated to No.7 VETERINARY HOSPITAL WB	
30-4-17	Nothing to report WB	
	One N.C.O and Three men Sent to Corps MOBILE VETERINARY DETACHMENT for duty WB	

O.C. 19th Mobile Veterinary Section

Secret

Vol 4 WAR DIARY

For the Month of MAY 1917

O.C. 19th Mobile Veterinary Section

WAR DIARY
or
INTELLIGENCE SUMMARY
(Erase heading not required.)

Army Form C. 2118.

Hour, Date, Place	Summary of Events and Information	Remarks and references to Appendices
1-5-17 HALLE	Nothing to report. WPS	
2-5-17 "	Nothing to report. WPS	
3-5-17 BOIRE	Section moved to Boire. WPS	
4-5-17 "	Six sick animals evacuated to O.C. N° South Mid. Mobile Vety Section LPS	
5-5-17 "	One man admitted to Field Ambulance. WPS	
6-5-17 "	Thirty one sick animals evacuated to N°7 Veterinary Hospital. WPS	
7-5-17 "	Nothing to report. WPS	
8-5-17 "	Nothing to report. WPS	
9-5-17 MARQUDIX	Six sick animals evacuated to N°7 Veterinary Hospital. WPS	
10-5-17 "	Section moved to Marguria. WPS	
11-5-17 "	One man reported from Field Ambulance. WPS	
12-5-17 "	Nothing to report. WPS	
13-5-17 "	Florida sick animals evacuated to N°7 Veterinary Hospital. WPS	
	One man sent to Base Depot for Dental treatment. WPS	
	One Driver A.S.C. reported from Base Depot for duty. WPS	
14-5-17 "	Nothing to report. WPS	
15-5-17 "	Thirty nine sick animals evacuated to N°7 Veterinary Hospital. WPS	
16-5-17 "	Nothing to report. WPS	
17-5-17 "	Nothing to report. WPS	
18-5-17 "	One R.C.O. and three men reported their arrival from Corps Mobile Veterinary Detachment. WPS	
19-5-17 "	Eighteen sick animals evacuated to N°7 Mobile Veterinary Section. WPS	
20-5-17 "	Two Drivers transferred to N°7 Veterinary Hospital. WPS	
21-5-17 ROEQUIEN	Section moved to Roequien. WPS	
22-5-17 "	Nothing to report. WPS	
23-5-17 "	One N.C.O. and three men reported to Corps Mobile Veterinary Detachment for duty. WPS	
24-5-17 "	Nothing to report. WPS	
25-5-17 "	Nothing to report. WPS	
26-5-17 "	Nothing to report. WPS	
27-5-17 "	Nothing to report. WPS	
29-5-17 "	Nothing to report. WPS	
30 "	One man returned to Base Depot as permanently unfit for service at the front. WPS	
31 "	Sick animals evacuated to N°7 Veterinary Hospital. WPS	
	Nothing to report approved to Field Ambulance. WPS	

O.B.19 Mobile Veterinary Section

Confidential
Vol 5

WAR DIARY

For the Month of June 1917

O. C. 19th Mobile Veterinary Section.

Vol. VI

WAR DIARY or INTELLIGENCE SUMMARY

(Erase heading not required.)

Army Form C. 2118.

Instructions regarding War Diaries and Intelligence Summaries are contained in F. S. Regs., Part II. and the Staff Manual respectively. Title pages will be prepared in manuscript.

Hour, Date, Place	Summary of Events and Information	Remarks and references to Appendices
1-6-17 ROCQUIGNY	Nothing to report. WRS	
2-6-17 "	Nothing to report. WRS	
3-6-17 "	One man reported his arrival for duty from No 4 VETERINARY HOSPITAL. WRS	
4-6-17 "	Two horses sent to FIELD REMOUNT DEPOT (authority A.D.V.S. FOURTH ARMY) WRS	
5-6-17 "	Eleven sick animals and seven animals cast for use evacuated to No 9 VETERINARY HOSPITAL. WRS	
6-6-17 "	Nothing to report. WRS	
7-6-17 "	Nothing to report. WRS	
8-6-17 "	Nothing to report. WRS	
9-6-17 "	Nothing to report. WRS	
10-6-17 "	Nothing to report. WRS	
11-6-17 "	Nothing to report. WRS	
12-6-17 "	Nothing to report. WRS	
13-6-17 "	One man reported his arrival from No 14 VETERINARY HOSPITAL. WRS Fourteen sick animals evacuated to No 9 VETERINARY HOSPITAL. WRS	
14-6-17 "	Nothing to report. WRS	
15-6-17 "	Nothing to report. WRS	
16-6-17 "	No.5339 Private Sargent appointed A/F/Sgt to complete War Establishment. WRS	
17-6-17 "	Nothing to report. WRS	
18-6-17 "	Nothing to report. WRS	
19-6-17 "	Nothing to report. WRS	
20-6-17 "	One man reported his arrival for duty from detached duty with No 2 Coy A.S.C. WRS	
21-6-17 "	Nothing to report. WRS	
22-6-17 "	No. 1268 Pte MANSFIELD.O.G. appointed A/F/Sgt to complete War Establishment. WRS	
23-6-17 "	Nothing to report. WRS	
24-6-17 "	Real sick animals evacuated to No 9 VETERINARY HOSPITAL. WRS	
25-6-17 "	Nothing to report. WRS	
26-6-17 "	Nothing to report. WRS	
27-6-17 "	Nothing to report. WRS	
28-6-17 "	Nothing to report. WRS	
29-6-17 "	Nothing to report. WRS	
30-6-17 "	Ten sick animals evacuated to No 9 VETERINARY HOSPITAL. WRS	

W. R. S. Clarke
O.C. 19th Mobile Veterinary Section

[Stamp: NO 19 MOBILE VETERINARY SECTION 30/6/17]

WAR DIARY.

For Month of July 1917

OC 19" Mobile Veterinary Section.

Army Form C. 2118.

WAR DIARY
or
INTELLIGENCE SUMMARY

(Erase heading not required.)

Instructions regarding War Diaries and Intelligence Summaries are contained in F. S. Regs., Part II. and the Staff Manual respectively. Title pages will be prepared in manuscript.

Hour, Date, Place	Summary of Events and Information	Remarks and references to Appendices
1-7-17 ROCQUIGNY	One Man reported for duty arrived from No 14 VETERINARY HOSPITAL M.B.	
2-7-17	Nothing to report. M.B.	
3-7-17	One man admitted to FIELD AMBULANCE. M.B.	
4-7-17	Nothing to report. M.B.	
5-7-17	Nothing to report. M.B.	
6-7-17	Nothing to report. M.B.	
7-7-17	Fourteen sick animals evacuated to No 7 VETERINARY HOSPITAL. M.B.	
8-7-17	Nothing to report. M.B.	
9-7-17	Section moved to ACHIET le PETIT. M.B.	
3pm ACHIET le Petit	Section arrived M.B.	
10-7-17	One Corporal and three privates reported their arrival from CORPS MOBILE VETERINARY DETACHMENT. M.B.	
11-7-17	Nothing to report. M.B.	
12-7-17	Nothing to report. M.B.	
13-7-17	One man reported for duty from FIELD AMBULANCE. M.B.	
14-7-17	Nothing to report. M.B.	
15-7-17	Nothing to report. M.B.	
16-7-17	Nothing to report. M.B.	
17-7-17	Twenty seven sick animals evacuated to No 7 VETERINARY HOSPITAL. M.B.	
18-7-17	Nothing to report. M.B.	
19-7-17	Nothing to report. M.B.	
20-7-17	Nothing to report. M.B.	
21-7-17	Nothing to report. M.B.	
22-7-17	Nothing to report. M.B.	
23-7-17	Nothing to report. M.B.	
24-7-17	Twenty seven sick animals evacuated to No 7 VETERINARY HOSPITAL M.B.	
25-7-17	Nothing to report. M.B.	
26-7-17	Nothing to report. M.B.	
27-7-17	Nothing to report. M.B.	
28-7-17	Nothing to report. M.B.	
29-7-17	Nothing to report. M.B.	
30-7-17	Nothing to report. M.B.	
31-7-17	Fifteen sick animals evacuated to No 7 Veterinary Hospital M.B.	W.P. Sykes Capt AVC OC 19th Mobile Veterinary Section

Confidential

Vol 7 War Diary.

Month August 1917.

OC 19 Mobile Veterinary Section.

WAR DIARY or INTELLIGENCE SUMMARY

Army Form C. 2118.

(Erase heading not required.)

Hour, Date, Place		Summary of Events and Information	Remarks and references to Appendices
1-8-17	ACHIET le PETIT	Nothing to report. W.R.S	
2-8-17	"	Nothing to report. W.R.S	
3-8-17	"	Nothing to report. W.R.S	
4-8-17	"	Nothing to report. W.R.S	
5-8-17	"	Nothing to report. W.R.S	
6-8-17	"	Nothing to report. W.R.S	
7-8-17	"	Fifteen sick animals evacuated to No 7 VETERINARY HOSPITAL. W.R.S	
8-8-17	"	Nothing to report. W.R.S	
9-8-17	"	Nothing to report. W.R.S	
10-8-17	"	Twenty sick animals evacuated to No 7 VETERINARY HOSPITAL. W.R.S	
11-8-17	"	Nothing to report. W.R.S	
12-8-17	"	Nothing to report. W.R.S	
13-8-17	"	Nothing to report. W.R.S	
14-8-17	"	Nothing to report. W.R.S	
15-8-17	"	Nothing to report. W.R.S	
16-8-17	"	Nothing to report. W.R.S	
17-8-17	"	Fourteen sick animals evacuated to No 7 VETERINARY HOSPITAL. W.R.S	
18-8-17	"	Nothing to report. W.R.S	
19-8-17	"	Nothing to report. W.R.S	
20-8-17	"	Nothing to report. W.R.S	
21-8-17	"	Nothing to report. W.R.S	
22-8-17	"	According to instructions received from D.A.D.V.S. 42" DIVISION. SECTION W.R.S Moved to AVELUY. W.R.S	
1 pm	AVELUY	Arrived. W.R.S	
12 Noon 23-8-17	ALBERT	SECTION moved to ALBERT. W.R.S Detained. W.R.S	
12 pm	GODEWAERWELDE	Detrained and marched to WATOU. W.R.S	
24-8-17	WATOU	Reported arrival to D.A.D.V.S. and took over CAMP Sheet 27, K18, B62. W.R.S	
25-8-17	"	Moved SECTION to map ref Sheet 27, M5, D86. One man admitted to FIELD AMBULANCE. One N.C.O. and three men posted to XIX CORPS, MOBILE, VETERINARY, DETACHMENT. W.R.S	
26-8-17	"	Nothing to report. W.R.S	
27-8-17	"	Nothing to report. W.R.S	
28-8-17	"	Two sick animals evacuated to XIX CORPS, MOBILE, VETERINARY, DETACHMENT. W.R.S	
29-8-17	"	Five sick animals evacuated to XIX CORPS, MOBILE, VETERINARY, DETACHMENT. W.R.S	
30-8-17	"	Nothing to report. W.R.S	
31-8-17	"	According to instructions received from D.A.D.V.S. 42" DIVISION. SECTION moved my SHEET 28 G.14. G.5.4. and took over CAMP from O.C. 27th Mobile Vet Section.	

Maps 57d.E.7.28.31.8.14 / G.5.14 / Forms C.2118/11 / XII. V.S.

to Major Cottance 19 Mobile Section
OC 19 Mobile Section

Confidential

Vol 8

WAR DIARY.

For the month ending September 1917.

O.C. 19th Mobile Veterinary Section.

Vol IX

WAR DIARY
or
INTELLIGENCE SUMMARY

(Erase heading not required.)

Army Form C. 2118.

Instructions regarding War Diaries and Intelligence Summaries are contained in F. S. Regs., Part II. and the Staff Manual respectively. Title pages will be prepared in manuscript.

Hour, Date, Place	Summary of Events and Information	Remarks and references to Appendices
1-9-17. POPERINGHE	Six sick animals evacuated to XIX Corps, Mobile, Veterinary, Detachment. L.P.S.	
2-9-17. "	Nothing to report. L.P.S.	
3-9-17. "	Twenty three sick animals evacuated to 28th Veterinary Hospital. L.P.S.	
4-9-17. "	One Staff Sergt reported their arrival for duty to complete War Establishment. L.P.S.	
5-9-17. "	Thirty one sick animals evacuated to XIX Corps, Mobile, Veterinary, Detachment. W.B.	
6-9-17. "	Nothing to report. L.P.S.	
7-9-17. "	One man admitted to Hospital. L.P.S.	
8-9-17. "	Nothing to report. L.P.S.	
9-9-17. "	Nothing to report. L.P.S.	
10-9-17. "	Nothing to report. L.P.S.	
11-9-17. "	Nothing to report. L.P.S.	
12-9-17. "	One N.C.O. and two men temporarily transferred to A10 Post. L.P.S.	
13-9-17. "	Nothing to report. L.P.S.	
14-9-17. "	One man reported their arrival for duty from No.2 Veterinary Hospital, L.P.S.	
15-9-17. "	Forty nine sick animals evacuated to XIX Corps, Mobile, Veterinary, Detachment. L.P.O.	
16-9-17. "	Nothing to report. L.P.S.	
17-9-17. "	Nothing to report. L.P.S.	
18-9-17. "	Nothing to report. L.P.S.	
19-9-17. "	Nothing to report. L.P.S.	
"	One N.C.O. and two men returned from A10 Post. L.P.S.	
"	Forty three sick animals transferred to O.C. 21st Mobile, Veterinary, Section. L.P.S.	
20-9-17. WINNEZEELE	According to instructions received from D.A.D.V.S. 42nd Division, Section moved to Winnezeele. L.P.S.	
"	One N.C.O. and two men returned from XIX Corps, Mobile, Veterinary, Detachment. L.P.S.	
21-9-17. "	Two men reported their arrival for duty from No.2 Veterinary Hospital. L.P.S.	
22-9-17. WORMHOUDT.	According to instructions received from 42nd Division, Section moved to Wormhoudt. L.P.S.	
23-9-17. LA PANNE	Section moved to La Panne. L.P.S.	
24-9-17. "	Nothing to report. L.P.S.	
25-9-17. "	Nothing to report. L.P.S.	
26-9-17. COXYDE BAINS	Section moved to Coxyde Bains. L.P.S.	
"	One N.C.O. and three men sent to XV Corps, Mobile, Veterinary, Detachment. L.P.S.	

W.T.Jones Capt. A.V.C.
O.C. 19th Mobile Veterinary Section

[Stamp: 19th MOBILE VETERINARY SECTION No. ... Date 30/9/17]

WAR DIARY
or
INTELLIGENCE SUMMARY

(Erase heading not required.)

Army Form C. 2118.

Hour, Date, Place	Summary of Events and Information	Remarks and references to Appendices
27.9.17 COXYDE BAINS	Nothing to report. A.M & P.M.	
28.9.17 "	Nothing to report.	
29.9.17 SAINT IDESBALD	According to instructions received from D.D.D.V.S. 42nd DIVISION. SECTION moved from to SAINT IDESBALD. W.R.	
30.9.17 " "	Nothing to report. A.M & P.M.	

J R Stokes Capt R.V.C.
O.C. 19th Mobile Veterinary Section

Confidential

WAR DIARY

For the month ending October 1917.

O.C. 19th Mobile Veterinary Section

Vol VII

Army Form C. 2118.

WAR DIARY
or
INTELLIGENCE SUMMARY

(Erase heading not required.)

Instructions regarding War Diaries and Intelligence Summaries are contained in F.S. Regs., Part II. and the Staff Manual respectively. Title pages will be prepared in manuscript.

Hour, Date, Place	Summary of Events and Information	Remarks and references to Appendices
1-10-17 ST. IDESBALD	Nothing to report. LPS	
2-10-17 "	Seventy Seven sick animals evacuated to No4 VETERINARY HOSPITAL. LPS.	
3-10-17 "	Nothing to report. LPS	
4-10-17 "	Nothing to report. LPS	
5-10-17 "	Nothing to report. LPS	
6-10-17 "	One N.C.O. withdrawn from XV CORPS, MOBILE VETERINARY DETACHMENT, and one man appointed unpaid acting corporal to replace N.C.O. temporarily. LPS	
7-10-17 Wed 24 w/18	Section moved to COXYDE. (JA)	
8-10-17 C.S.Y.	One N.C.O. sent to No2 VETERINARY HOSPITAL for duty. LPS.	
9-10-17 "	Twenty nine sick animals evacuated to No4 VETERINARY HOSPITAL. LA	
10-10-17 "	One A.S.C. Driver Surplus to Establishment transferred to 42nd DIVISIONAL TRAIN. LPS.	
" "	One man admitted to HOSPITAL. LPS	
11-10-17 "	One reinforcement received from No4 VETERINARY HOSPITAL. LM	
12-10-17 "	Nothing to report. LPS	
13-10-17 "	Nothing to report. LPS	
14-10-17 "	Nothing to report. LPS	
15-10-17 "	Nothing to report. LM	
16-10-17 "	Twenty four sick animals evacuated to No4 VETERINARY HOSPITAL. LPS	
17-10-17 "	Nothing to report. LPS	
18-10-17 "	Nothing to report. LA	
19-10-17 "	Nothing to report. LPS	
20-10-17 "	Nothing to report. L.A	
21-10-17 "	Nothing to report. LA	
22-10-17 "	Fourteen men reported their arrival for duty (to replace Category A men) from No6 VETERINARY HOSPITAL. LPS	
" "	Three men withdrawn from XV CORPS, MOBILE VETERINARY DETACHMENT, replaced by three others. LPS	
23-10-17 "	Eleven Category A men transferred to No2 VETERINARY HOSPITAL. LPS	
" "	Twenty three sick animals evacuated to No4 VETERINARY HOSPITAL. LPS.	
24-10-17 "	One man reported his arrival from HOSPITAL. LPS.	
25-10-17 "	One Category A man transferred to No2 VETERINARY HOSPITAL. LPS	
26-10-17 "	Nothing to report. LPS	
27-10-17 "	One Category A man transferred to No2 VETERINARY HOSPITAL. LPS.	
28-10-17 "	Nothing to report. LPS	
29-10-17 "	Nothing to report. LP.	
30-10-17 "	Thirty nine sick animals evacuated to No4 VETERINARY HOSPITAL	
31-10-17 "	Nothing to report. LP	

Vol 10

WAR DIARY

For the month of November 1917

O.C. 19th Mobile Veterinary Section

Army Form C. 2118.

WAR DIARY
or
INTELLIGENCE SUMMARY
(Erase heading not required.)

Instructions regarding War Diaries and Intelligence Summaries are contained in F. S. Regs., Part II. and the Staff Manual respectively. Title pages will be prepared in manuscript.

Hour, Date, Place		Summary of Events and Information	Remarks and references to Appendices
1-11-17	COXYDE	One reinforcement reported his arrival from No 2 VETERINARY HOSPITAL. WRS	
2-11-17	"	One bay pony A. MOSS transferred to No 2 VETERINARY HOSPITAL. WRS	
3-11-17	"	Nothing to report. WRS	
4-11-17	"	Nothing to report. WRS	
5-11-17	"	Nothing to report. WRS	
6-11-17	"	Seven sick animals evacuated to No 4 VETERINARY HOSPITAL. WRS	
7-11-17	"	Nothing to report. WRS	
8-11-17	"	Nothing to report. WRS	
9-11-17	"	Nothing to report. WRS	
10-11-17	"	Nothing to report. WRS	
11-11-17	"	Nothing to report. WRS	
12-11-17	"	Nothing to report. WRS	
13-11-17	"	Eleven Bay sick animals evacuated to No 4 VETERINARY HOSPITAL. WRS	
14-11-17	"	Nothing to report. WRS	
15-11-17	"	Nothing to report. WRS	
16-11-17	"	Nothing to report. WRS	
17-11-17	"	Nothing to report. WRS	
18-11-17	"	Nothing to report. WRS	
19-11-17	"	Four men reported their arrival from CORPS MOBILE VETERINARY DETACHMENT. WRS	
20-11-17	"	Twenty two sick animals evacuated to No 4 VETERINARY HOSPITAL. WRS	
21-11-17	"	One sick animal evacuated to XV CORPS MOBILE VETERINARY DETACHMENT. WRS	
22-11-17	GHYVELDE	Section moved to GHYVELDE. WRS	
23-11-17	WORMHOUDT	Section moved to WORMHOUDT. WRS	
24-11-17	ZERMEZEELE	Section moved to ZERMEZEELE. WRS	
25-11-17	HOUDEGHAM	Section moved to HOUDEGHAM. WRS	
26-11-17	LAMBRES	Section moved to LAMBRES. WRS	
27-11-17	"	Nothing to report. WRS	
28-11-17	"	Four sick animals evacuated to No 22 VETERINARY HOSPITAL. WRS	
29-11-17	ESSARS	Section moved to ESSARS, and took over CAMP from O.C. 37th MOBILE VETERINARY SECTION. WRS	
30-11-17	"	Nothing to report. WRS	

W.R.Stokes
Capt AVC
O/c 19th Mobile Veterinary Section

Army Form C. 2118.

WAR DIARY
or
INTELLIGENCE SUMMARY
(Erase heading not required.)

Instructions regarding War Diaries and Intelligence Summaries are contained in F. S. Regs., Part II. and the Staff Manual respectively. Title pages will be prepared in manuscript.

Hour, Date, Place	Summary of Events and Information	Remarks and references to Appendices
1-11-17 COXYDE	One reinforcement reported for arrival from No 2 VETERINARY HOSPITAL. A/R	
2-11-17	One Category B H.915 transferred to No 2 VETERINARY HOSPITAL. A/R	
3-11-17	Nothing to report. A/R	
4-11-17	Nothing to report. A/R	
5-11-17	Nothing to report. A/R	
6-11-17	Casualty Sick animals evacuated to No.4 VETERINARY HOSPITAL. G/R	
7-11-17	Nothing to report. A/R	
8-11-17	Nothing to report. A/R	
9-11-17	Nothing to report. A/R	
10-11-17	Nothing to report. A/R	
11-11-17	Nothing to report. A/R	
12-11-17	Nothing to report. A/R	
13-11-17	Veterinary Sick animals to evacuate to No 4 VETERINARY HOSPITAL. L/R	
14-11-17	Nothing to report. A/R	
15-11-17	Nothing to report. A/R	
16-11-17	Nothing to report. A/R	
17-11-17	Nothing to report. A/R	
18-11-17	Nothing to report. A/R	
19-11-17	Nothing to report. A/R	
20-11-17	Four Reg reported their arrival from CORPS MOBILE VETERINARY DETACHMENT L/R	
21-11-17	Twenty Two Sick animals evacuated to No 4 VETERINARY HOSPITAL. L/R	
22-11-17 GHYVELDE	One Sick animal evacuated to XV CORPS MOBILE VETERINARY DETACHMENT L/R Section moved to GHYVELDE L/R	
23-11-17 WORMHOUDT	Section moved to WORMHOUDT. A/R	
24-11-17 ZERMEZEELE	Section moved to ZERMEZEELE. L/R	
25-11-17 HOUDEGHAN	Section moved to HOUDEGHAM. L/R	
26-11-17 LAMBRES	Section moved to LAMBRES. L/R	
27-11-17	Nothing to report. A/R	
28-11-17	One Sick animal evacuated to No 22 VETERINARY HOSPITAL. L/R	
29-11-17 ESSARS	Section moved to ESSARS, and took over camp from O.C. 37th MOBILE VETERINARY SECTION. A/R	
30-11-17	Nothing to report. A/R	

J.M. Miles Capt.
O.C. 19th Mobile Veterinary Section

WAR DIARY

For the Month ending December 1914.

O/c 19th Mobile Veterinary Section

Army Form C. 2118.

WAR DIARY
or
INTELLIGENCE SUMMARY

(Erase heading not required.)

Instructions regarding War Diaries and Intelligence Summaries are contained in F. S. Regs., Part II. and the Staff Manual respectively. Title pages will be prepared in manuscript.

Hour, Date, Place	Summary of Events and Information	Remarks and references to Appendices
1-12-17 ESSARS	Nothing to report. LPS	
2-12-17 "	Nothing to report. LPS	
3-12-17 "	Nothing to report. LPS	
4-12-17 "	One Other Rank SURPLUS TO ESTABLISHMENT sent to No 2 VETERINARY HOSPITAL. LW	
5-12-17 "	Nothing to report. LPS	
6-12-17 "	Nothing to report. LPS	
7-12-17 "	Nothing to report. LPS	
8-12-17 "	Nothing to report. LPS	
9-12-17 "	Nothing to report. LPS	
10-12-17 "	Nothing to report. LPS	
11-12-17 "	Thirty six sick animals evacuated to No 22 VETERINARY HOSPITAL. LPS	
12-12-17 "	Nothing to report. LPS	
13-12-17 "	Nothing to report. LPS	
14-12-17 "	Thirty one sick animals evacuated to No 22 VETERINARY HOSPITAL. LPS	
15-12-17 "	Nothing to report. LPS	
16-12-17 "	Nothing to report. LPS	
17-12-17 "	Camp inspected by D.D.V.S. FIRST ARMY. LPS	
18-12-17 "	Nothing to report. LPS	
19-12-17 "	Thirty nine sick animals evacuated to No 14 VETERINARY HOSPITAL. LPS	
20-12-17 "	Twenty one sick animals evacuated to No 23 VETERINARY HOSPITAL. LPS	
21-12-17 "	Nothing to report. LPS	
22-12-17 "	Nothing to report. LPS	
23-12-17 "	Fifteen sick animals evacuated to No 14 VETERINARY HOSPITAL. LPS	
24-12-17 "	Eighteen sick animals evacuated to No 23 VETERINARY HOSPITAL. LPS	
25-12-17 "	Nothing to report. LPS	
26-12-17 "	Nothing to report. LPS	
27-12-17 "	Nothing to report. LPS	
28-12-17 "	Twelve sick animals evacuated to No 23 VETERINARY HOSPITAL. LPS	
29-12-17 "	Nothing to report. LPS	
30-12-17 "	Nothing to report. LPS	
31-12-17 "	Nothing to report. LPS	

Army Form C. 2118.

WAR DIARY
or
INTELLIGENCE SUMMARY
(Erase heading not required.)

Hour, Date, Place	Summary of Events and Information	Remarks and references to Appendices
1-12-17 ESSARS	Nothing to report. 670	
2-12-17	Nothing to report. 685	
3-12-17	Nothing to report. 685	
4-12-17	One other Ranks sick/lame sent to No 22 Veterinary Hospital 684	
5-12-17	Nothing to report. 685	
6-12-17	Nothing to report. 685	
7-12-17	Nothing to report. 685	
8-12-17	Nothing to report. 685	
9-12-17	Nothing to report. 685	
10-12-17	Three sick animals evacuated to No 22 Veterinary Hospital 685	
11-12-17	Nothing to report. 7/AM	
12-12-17	Nothing to report.	
13-12-17	Nothing to report.	
14-12-17	Two sick animals evacuated to No 22 Veterinary Hospital 678	
15-12-17	Nothing to report. 678	
16-12-17	Inspected by D.D.V.S. First Army. 678	
17-12-17	Nothing to report. 678	
18-12-17	Three sick animals evacuated to No 14 Veterinary Hospital 675	
19-12-17	Twenty one sick animals evacuated to No 22 Veterinary Hospital. 654	
20-12-17	Nothing to report. 654	
21-12-17	Nothing to report. 654	
22-12-17	Three sick animals evacuated to No 14 Veterinary Hospital. 650	
23-12-17	Sixteen sick animals evacuated to No 23 Veterinary Hospital. 635	
24-12-17	Nothing to report. 635	
25-12-17	Nothing to report. 635	
26-12-17	Nothing to report. 635	
27-12-17	Fourteen sick animals evacuated to No 23 Veterinary Hospital. 621	
28-12-17	Nothing to report. 621	
29-12-17	Nothing to report. 621	
30-12-17	Nothing to report. 621	
31-12-17	Nothing to report. 621	

Confidential

WAR DIARY

For the month of January 1918

Of 19th Mobile Veterinary Section

19 Mob Vety Sec
Feb 12

WAR DIARY
or
INTELLIGENCE SUMMARY

(Erase heading not required.)

Army Form C. 2118.

Hour, Date, Place	Summary of Events and Information	Remarks and references to Appendices
1-1-18. ESSARS.	Thirty sick animals evacuated to No.14 VETERINARY HOSPITAL. W.P.S	
2-1-18 "	Twenty eight sick animals evacuated to No.23 VETERINARY HOSPITAL. W.P.S	
3-1-18 "	Nothing to report. W.P.S	
4-1-18 "	Nothing to report. W.P.S	
5-1-18 "	Nothing to report. W.P.S	
6-1-18 "	Nothing to report. W.P.S	
7-1-18 "	Twenty six sick animals evacuated to No.23 VETERINARY HOSPITAL. W.P.S	
8-1-18 "	Nothing to report. W.P.S	
9-1-18 "	Fourteen sick animals evacuated to No.14 VETERINARY HOSPITAL. W.P.S	
10-1-18 "	Nothing to report. W.P.S	
11-1-18 "	Nothing to report. W.P.S	
12-1-18 "	Sixteen sick animals evacuated to No.23 VETERINARY HOSPITAL. W.P.S	
13-1-18 "	Nothing to report. W.P.S	
14-1-18 "	Nothing to report. W.P.S	
15-1-18 "	Nothing to report. W.P.S	
16-1-18 "	Sixteen sick animals evacuated to No.14 VETERINARY HOSPITAL. W.P.S	
17-1-18 "	Nothing to report. W.P.S	
18-1-18 "	Six sick animals evacuated to No.23 VETERINARY HOSPITAL. W.P.S	
19-1-18 "	Twenty eight sick animals evacuated to No.14 VETERINARY HOSPITAL. W.P.S	
20-1-18 "	Nothing to report. W.P.S	
21-1-18 "	Nothing to report. W.P.S	
22-1-18 "	Nothing to report. W.P.S	
23-1-18 "	Forty two sick animals evacuated to No.14 VETERINARY HOSPITAL. W.P.S	
24-1-18 "	One man admitted to FIELD AMBULANCE. W.P.S	
25-1-18 "	Nothing to report. W.P.S	
26-1-18 "	Twenty eight sick animals evacuated to No.14 VETERINARY HOSPITAL. W.P.S	
27-1-18 "	Five sick animals evacuated to No.23 VETERINARY HOSPITAL. W.P.S	
28-1-18 "	Nothing to report. W.P.S	
29-1-18 "	Nothing to report. W.P.S	
30-1-18 "	Ninety sick animals evacuated to No.14 VETERINARY HOSPITAL. W.P.S	31.1.18.
31-1-18 "	One man evacuated to FIELD AMBULANCE. W.P.S Twenty five sick animals evacuated to No.23 VETERINARY HOSPITAL. W.P.S	

W.P.Stokes Colonel
O.C. 9th Mobile Veterinary Section

Army Form C. 2118.

WAR DIARY
or
INTELLIGENCE SUMMARY

(Erase heading not required.)

Hour, Date, Place	Summary of Events and Information	Remarks and references to Appendices
1.1.18 ESSARS	Forty sick animals evacuated to No.14 VETERINARY HOSPITAL L/R	
2.1.18 "	Twenty eight sick animals evacuated to No.23 VETERINARY HOSPITAL L/R	
3.1.18 "	Nothing to report L/R	
4.1.18 "	Nothing to report L/R	
5.1.18 "	Nothing to report L/R	
6.1.18 "	Nothing to report L/R	
7.1.18 "	Forty six sick animals evacuated to No.23 VETERINARY HOSPITAL L/R	
8.1.18 "	Forty four sick animals evacuated to No.14 VETERINARY HOSPITAL L/R	
9.1.18 "	Nothing to report L/R	
10.1.18 "	Nothing to report L/R	
11.1.18 "	Thirty sick animals evacuated to No.23 VETERINARY HOSPITAL L/R	
12.1.18 "	Nothing to report L/R	
13.1.18 "	Nothing to report L/R	
14.1.18 "	Nothing to report L/R	
15.1.18 "	Thirty sick animals evacuated to No.14 VETERINARY HOSPITAL L/R	
16.1.18 "	Nothing to report L/R	
17.1.18 "	D.A.D.V.S. animals evacuated to No.14 VETERINARY HOSPITAL L/R	
18.1.18 "	Twenty eight sick animals evacuated to No.23 VETERINARY HOSPITAL L/R	
19.1.18 "	Nothing to report L/R	
20.1.18 "	Nothing to report L/R	
21.1.18 "	Nothing to report L/R	
22.1.18 "	Forty five sick animals evacuated to No.14 VETERINARY HOSPITAL L/R	
23.1.18 "	One man admitted to FIELD AMBULANCE L/R	
24.1.18 "	Nothing to report L/R	
25.1.18 "	Twenty eight sick animals evacuated to No.14 VETERINARY HOSPITAL L/R	
26.1.18 "	Six sick animals evacuated to No.23 VETERINARY HOSPITAL L/R	
27.1.18 "	Nothing to report L/R	
28.1.18 "	Nothing to report L/R	
29.1.18 "	Multiplied wounds evacuated to No.14 VETERINARY HOSPITAL L/R	
30.1.18 "	One man evacuated to FIELD AMBULANCE L/R	
31.1.18 "	Twenty five sick animals wounded to No.23 VETERINARY HOSPITAL L/R	

W.R. Stokes Capt.
O.C. 19th Mobile Veterinary Sec.

WAR DIARY

For the month of February 1918.

O.C. 19th Mobile Veterinary Section

WAR DIARY
or
INTELLIGENCE SUMMARY.
(Erase heading not required.)

Army Form C. 2118.

Place	Date	Hour	Summary of Events and Information	Remarks and references to Appendices
ESSARS	1-2-18		Nothing to report. WS	
"	2-2-18		Nothing to report. WS	
"	3-2-18		Nothing to report. WS	
"	4-2-18		Thirty eight sick animals evacuated to No.14 Veterinary Hospital. WS Fourteen sick animals evacuated to No.23 Veterinary Hospital. WS	
"	5-2-18		Nothing to report. WS	
"	6-2-18		Nothing to report. WS	
"	7-2-18		Thirty three sick animals evacuated to No.14 Veterinary Hospital. WS	
"	8-2-18		Nothing to report. WS	
"	9-2-18		Nothing to report. WS	
"	10-2-18		Forty sick animals evacuated to No.13 Veterinary Hospital. WS	
"	11-2-18		Nothing to report. WS	
"	12-2-18		Nothing to report. WS	
"	13-2-18		Nothing to report. WS	
"	14-2-18		Nothing to report. WS	
"	15-2-18		Sixty three sick animals evacuated to No.13 Veterinary Hospital. WS Section moved to HESDIGNEUL. WS	
"	16-2-18		Nothing to report. WS	
HESDIGNEUL	17-2-18		Nothing to report. WS	
"	18-2-18		Twenty sick animals evacuated to No.23 Veterinary Hospital. WS Ten sick animals evacuated to No.13 Veterinary Hospital. WS	
"	19-2-18		Nothing to report. WS	
"	20-2-18		Nothing to report. WS	
"	21-2-18		Sixteen sick animals evacuated to No.13 Veterinary Hospital. WS Fourteen sick animals evacuated to No.23 Veterinary Hospital. WS	
"	22-2-18		Nothing to report. WS	
"	23-2-18		No.533 P/P/Sgt. SCARCE E.F. tried by F.G.C.M. WS Sentence confirmed and promulgated 42 days F.P. No.1. WS	
"	24-2-18			
"	25-2-18		Sixteen sick animals evacuated to No.13 Veterinary Hospital. WS	
"	26-2-18			
"	27-2-18		Nine sick animals evacuated to No.23 Veterinary Hospital. WS	
"	28-2-18		Nothing to report. WS	

W. Stone Captain
O.C. 19th Mobile Veterinary Section

19th MOBILE VETERINARY SECTION
No. 2 Date 28/2/18

Army Form C. 2118.

WAR DIARY
or
INTELLIGENCE SUMMARY.
(Erase heading not required.)

Instructions regarding War Diaries and Intelligence Summaries are contained in F. S. Regs., Part II. and the Staff Manual respectively. Title pages will be prepared in manuscript.

Place	Date	Hour	Summary of Events and Information	Remarks and references to Appendices
ESSARS	1.2.18		To report	
"	2.2.18		To report	
"	3.2.18		To report	
"	4.2.18		2 sick animals evacuated to No. 10th Veterinary Hospital	
"	5.2.18		5 sick animals evacuated to No. 23 Veterinary Hospital	
"	6.2.18		To report	
"	7.2.18		To report	
"	8.2.18		4 sick animals evacuated to No. 4 Veterinary Hospital	
"	9.2.18		To report	
"	10.2.18		To report	
"	11.2.18		2 sick animals evacuated to No. 23 Veterinary Hospital	
"	12.2.18		To report	
"	13.2.18		To report	
"	14.2.18		To report	
"	15.2.18		To report	
"	16.2.18		Mobile Section moved to HESDIGNEUL	
HESDIGNEUL	17.2.18		To report	
"	18.2.18		To report	
"	19.2.18		2 sick animals evacuated to No. 23 Veterinary Hospital	
"	20.2.18		2 sick animals evacuated to No. 13 Veterinary Hospital	
"	21.2.18		To report	
"	22.2.18		To report	
"	23.2.18		2 sick animals evacuated to No. 23 Veterinary Hospital	
"	23.2.18		2 sick animals evacuated to No. 23 Veterinary Hospital	
"	23.2.18		To report	
"	24.2.18		Pte. SMITH Source I.E.F. tried by F.G.C.M.	
"	25.2.18		Pte. SMITH sentenced and promulgated 42 days F.P. no. 1	
"	26.2.18		3 sick animals evacuated to No. 13 Veterinary Hospital	
"	27.2.18		3 sick animals evacuated to No. 23 Veterinary Hospital	
"	28.2.18		Nothing to report	

Signed: [signature]
O.C. 19th Mobile Veterinary Section

WAR DIARY.

For the month ending March 1918.

O.C. 19th Mobile Veterinary Section.

Unit dismounted in France Feb 20th 1917.

Army Form C. 2118.

WAR DIARY
or
INTELLIGENCE SUMMARY.
(Erase heading not required.)

Instructions regarding War Diaries and Intelligence Summaries are contained in F. S. Regs., Part II. and the Staff Manual respectively. Title pages will be prepared in manuscript.

Place	Date	Hour	Summary of Events and Information	Remarks and references to Appendices
HESDIGNEUL	1-3-18		Seventeen sick animals evacuated to No 13 VETERINARY HOSPITAL. MP	
	2-3-18		One man discharged from FIELD AMBULANCE. MP	
	3-3-18		Nothing to report. MP	
	4-3-18		Six sick animals evacuated to No 23 VETERINARY HOSPITAL. MP	
	5-3-18		Nothing to report. MP	
	6-3-18		Nine sick animals evacuated to No 13 VETERINARY HOSPITAL. MP	
	7-3-18		Nothing to report. MP	
	8-3-18		Four sick animals evacuated to No 23 VETERINARY HOSPITAL. MP	
	9-3-18		Nothing to report. MP	
	10-3-18		Nothing to report. MP	
	11-3-18		Seventeen sick animals evacuated to No 13 VETERINARY HOSPITAL. MP	
	12-3-18		Nothing to report. MP	
	13-3-18		Eleven sick animals evacuated to No 13 VETERINARY HOSPITAL. MP	
	14-3-18		Nothing to report. MP	
	15-3-18		Nothing to report. MP	
	16-3-18		Six sick animals evacuated to No 23 VETERINARY HOSPITAL. MP	
	17-3-18		No SGS G'S' Health LP reported his arrival for duty from No 19 VETERINARY HOSPITAL. MP	
	18-3-18		Nine sick animals evacuated to No 23 VETERINARY HOSPITAL. MP	
	19-3-18		Nothing to report. MP	
	20-3-18		Nothing to report. MP	
	21-3-18		Nothing to report. MP	
	22-3-18		Seven sick animals evacuated to No 23 VETERINARY HOSPITAL. MP	
	23-3-18	5 am	According to instructions received from D.R.D.V.S. 42nd DIVISION, SECTION moved to TINCQUES. MP	
TINCQUES.		6 pm	Arrived at TINCQUES. MP	
	24-3-18	2:30 pm	SECTION moved to ABLAINZEVILLE. MP	
ABLAINZEVILLE	25-3-18	11:30 am	SECTION arrived at ABLAINZEVILLE. MP	
	25-3-18	8 am	SECTION moved to BEIN-VILLERS. MP	
BEIN-VILLERS.		5 pm	SECTION arrived at BEIN-VILLERS. MP	
	26-3-18	1 pm	SECTION moved to ST ARMAND. MP	
ST ARMAND.		2 pm	SECTION arrived at ST ARMAND. MP	
	27-3-18		Nothing to report. MP	
	28-3-18	8 am	SECTION moved to COUIN. MP	
COUIN		10 am	SECTION arrived at COUIN. MP	
	29-3-18		Nothing to report. MP	
	30-3-18		Thirty sick animals evacuated to No 13 VETERINARY HOSPITAL. MP	
	31-3-18		Nothing to report. MP	

[Stamp: 15th MOBILE VETERINARY SECTION 31/3/18]

O.C. 19th Mobile Veterinary Section

Army Form C. 2118.

WAR DIARY
or
INTELLIGENCE SUMMARY.

(Erase heading not required.)

Instructions regarding War Diaries and Intelligence Summaries are contained in F. S. Regs., Part II. and the Staff Manual respectively. Title pages will be prepared in manuscript.

Place	Date	Hour	Summary of Events and Information	Remarks and references to Appendices
HESDIGNEUL	1.3.18		Seventeen sick animals evacuated to No 13 VETERINARY HOSPITAL. MO	
"	2.3.18		One man discharged from FIELD AMBULANCE. WO	
"	3.3.18		Six sick animals evacuated to No 23 VETERINARY HOSPITAL. WO	
"	4.3.18		Nothing to report. WO	
"	5.3.18		Fourteen sick animals evacuated to No 13 VETERINARY HOSPITAL. WO	
"	6.3.18		Eight sick animals evacuated to No 23 VETERINARY HOSPITAL. WO	
"	7.3.18		Nothing to report. WO	
"	8.3.18		Nothing to report. WO	
"	9.3.18		Nothing to report. WO	
"	10.3.18		Nothing to report. WO	
"	11.3.18		Seventeen sick animals evacuated to No 13 VETERINARY HOSPITAL. WO	
"	12.3.18		Nothing to report. WO	
"	13.3.18		Fourteen sick animals evacuated to No 13 VETERINARY HOSPITAL. WO	
"	14.3.18		Nothing to report. WO	
"	15.3.18		Nothing to report. WO	
"	16.3.18		Six sick animals evacuated to No 23 VETERINARY HOSPITAL. WO	
"	17.3.18		No 5080 Sgt. Smith E.P. reported his arrival on duty from No 19 VETERINARY HOSPITAL. WO	
"	18.3.18		Nine sick animals evacuated to No 23 VETERINARY HOSPITAL. WO	
"	19.3.18		Nothing to report. WO	
"	20.3.18		Nothing to report. WO	
"	21.3.18		Nothing to report. WO	
"	22.3.18		Seven sick animals evacuated to No 23 VETERINARY HOSPITAL. WO	
"	23.3.18	5 am	According to instructions received from D.A.D.V.S. 42nd DIVISION, SECTION moved to TINCQUES. WO	
TINCQUES	24.3.18	6pm	Arrived at TINCQUES. WO	
"	24.3.18	7.30pm	SECTION moved to ABLAINZEVILLE. WO	
ABLAINZEVILLE	25.3.18	4.30am	SECTION arrived at ABLAINZEVILLE. WO	
"	25.3.18	8 am	SECTION moved to BEIN-VILLERS. WO	
BEIN-VILLERS	"	5pm	SECTION arrived at BEIN-VILLERS. WO	
"	26.3.18	1 pm	SECTION moved to ST AMAND. WO	
ST AMAND	"	2pm	SECTION arrived at ST AMAND. WO	
"	27.3.18		Nothing to report. WO	
"	28.3.18	8am	SECTION moved to COUIN. WO	
COUIN	"	10am	SECTION arrived at COUIN. WO	
"	29.3.18		Nothing to report. WO	
"	30.3.18		Thirty sick animals evacuated to No 23 VETERINARY HOSPITAL. WO	
"	31.3.18		Nothing to report. WO	

WAR DIARY.

For the month ending APRIL 1918.

O.C. 19th Mobile Veterinary Section.

Army Form C. 2118.

WAR DIARY
or
INTELLIGENCE SUMMARY.
(Erase heading not required.)

Instructions regarding War Diaries and Intelligence Summaries are contained in F. S. Regs., Part II. and the Staff Manual respectively. Title pages will be prepared in manuscript.

Place	Date	Hour	Summary of Events and Information	Remarks and references to Appendices
COUIN	1.4.18		Twenty two sick animals evacuated to No 18 VETERINARY HOSPITAL. WM	
—	2.4.18	1 PM	Section moved to SOUASTRE. WM	
SOUASTRE	—	2 PM	Section arrived at SOUASTRE. WM	
—	3.4.18		Eighteen sick animals evacuated to V CORPS VETERINARY EVACUATION STATION. WM	
—	4.4.18		Twenty five sick animals evacuated to V CORPS VETERINARY EVACUATION STATION. WM	
—	5.4.18		One man admitted to FIELD AMBULANCE. WM	
—	6.4.18		Forty seven sick animals evacuated to IV CORPS VETERINARY EVACUATION STATION. WM	
—	7.4.18	3 PM	Twenty four sick animals evacuated to IV CORPS VETERINARY EVACUATION STATION. WM	
—	—	4.30 PM	Section moved to PAS. WM	
PAS	—		Section arrived at PAS. WM	
—	8.4.18		Nine sick animals evacuated to IV CORPS VETERINARY EVACUATION STATION. WM	
—	9.4.18		Party to report. WM	
—	10.4.18		Thirty one sick animals evacuated to IV CORPS VETERINARY EVACUATION STATION. WM	
—	11.4.18		Thirteen sick animals evacuated to V CORPS VETERINARY EVACUATION STATION. WM	
—	12.4.18		Fourteen sick animals evacuated to IV CORPS VETERINARY EVACUATION STATION. WM	
—	13.4.18		One sick animal evacuated to IV CORPS VETERINARY EVACUATION STATION. WM	
—	14.4.18		Six sick animals evacuated to IV CORPS VETERINARY EVACUATION STATION. WM	
—	—	6 AM	Section moved to BOIS du ST PIERRE. WM	
BOIS du ST PIERRE	—	7 AM	Section arrived at BOIS du ST PIERRE. WM	
—	15.4.18		Nothing to report. WM	
—	16.4.18		Seventy two sick animals evacuated to IV CORPS VETERINARY EVACUATION STATION. WM	
—	17.4.18		Twenty three sick animals evacuated to IV CORPS VETERINARY EVACUATION STATION. WM	
—	18.4.18		Six sick animals evacuated to V CORPS VETERINARY EVACUATION STATION. WM	
—	19.4.18		Fifteen sick animals evacuated to IV CORPS VETERINARY EVACUATION STATION. WM	
—	20.4.18		Fourteen sick animals evacuated to IV CORPS VETERINARY EVACUATION STATION. WM	
—	21.4.18		Twenty two sick animals evacuated to IV CORPS VETERINARY EVACUATION STATION. WM	
—	22.4.18		Seven sick animals evacuated to IV CORPS VETERINARY EVACUATION STATION. WM	
—	23.4.18		Nineteen sick animals evacuated to IV CORPS VETERINARY EVACUATION STATION. WM	
—	24.4.18		Twelve sick animals evacuated to IV CORPS VETERINARY EVACUATION STATION. WM	
—	25.4.18		Twelve sick animals evacuated to V CORPS VETERINARY EVACUATION STATION. WM	
—	26.4.18		Thirteen sick animals evacuated to V CORPS VETERINARY EVACUATION STATION. WM	
—	27.4.18		Eight sick animals evacuated to V CORPS VETERINARY EVACUATION STATION. WM	
—	—		One man admitted from No 2 VETERINARY HOSPITAL for duty. WM	
—	28.4.18		One man rejoined his unit from No 14 VETERINARY HOSPITAL for further training. WM	
—	29.4.18		One man admitted from No 14 VETERINARY HOSPITAL for duty. WM	
—	—		Eight sick animals evacuated to V CORPS VETERINARY EVACUATION STATION. WM	
—	—		Six sick animals evacuated to V CORPS VETERINARY EVACUATION STATION. WM	
—	30.4.18		Eleven sick animals transferred to V CORPS VETERINARY EVACUATION STATION. WM	

W. Stokes Capt. AVC
O.C. 19th Mobile Veterinary Section

Army Form C. 2118.

WAR DIARY
or
INTELLIGENCE SUMMARY.

(Erase heading not required.)

Place	Date	Hour	Summary of Events and Information	Remarks and references to Appendices
COUIN	1.4.18		Twenty two sick animals evacuated to No13 Veterinary Hospital. WM	
	2.4.18	1 pm	Section moved to Souastre. WM	
SOUASTRE	3.4.18	2 pm	Section arrived at Souastre. WM	
	3.4.18		Eighteen sick animals evacuated to II Corps Veterinary Evacuation Station. WM	
	4.4.18		Twenty five sick animals evacuated to II Corps Veterinary Evacuation Station. WM	
	5.4.18		One man admitted to Field Ambulance. WM	
	6.4.18		Forty seven sick animals evacuated to IV Corps Veterinary Evacuation Station. WM	
	7.4.18	3 pm	Thirty four sick animals evacuated to IV Corps Veterinary Evacuation Station. WM	
	7.4.18	4:30 pm	Section moved to Pas. WM	
PAS	8.4.18		Section arrived at Pas. WM	
	8.4.18		Nine sick animals evacuated to IV Corps Veterinary Evacuation Station. WM	
	9.4.18		Nothing to report. WM	
	10.4.18		Thirty one sick animals evacuated to IV Corps Veterinary Evacuation Station. WM	
	11.4.18		Fifteen sick animals evacuated to IV Corps Veterinary Evacuation Station. WM	
	12.4.18		Thirteen sick animals evacuated to IV Corps Veterinary Evacuation Station. WM	
	13.4.18		One sick animal evacuated to IV Corps Veterinary Evacuation Station. WM	
	14.4.18		Section moved to Bois de St Pierre. WM	
BOIS du ST PIERRE	15.4.18	6 am	Section arrived at Bois de St Pierre. WM	
	15.4.18	7 am	Nothing to report. WM	
	16.4.18		Twenty five sick animals evacuated to IV Corps Veterinary Evacuation Station. WM	
	17.4.18		Thirty three sick animals evacuated to IV Corps Veterinary Evacuation Station. WM	
	18.4.18		Six sick animals evacuated to IV Corps Veterinary Evacuation Station. WM	
	19.4.18		Three sick animals evacuated to IV Corps Veterinary Evacuation Station. WM	
	20.4.18		Fourteen sick animals evacuated to IV Corps Veterinary Evacuation Station. WM	
	21.4.18		Twenty two sick animals evacuated to IV Corps Veterinary Evacuation Station. WM	
	22.4.18		Eleven sick animals evacuated to IV Corps Veterinary Evacuation Station. WM	
	23.4.18		Nineteen sick animals evacuated to IV Corps Veterinary Evacuation Station. WM	
	24.4.18		Twelve sick animals evacuated to IV Corps Veterinary Evacuation Station. WM	
	25.4.18		Twelve sick animals evacuated to IV Corps Veterinary Evacuation Station. WM	
	26.4.18		Fourteen sick animals evacuated to IV Corps Veterinary Evacuation Station. WM	
	27.4.18		Thirteen sick animals evacuated to IV Corps Veterinary Evacuation Station. WM	
	28.4.18		One man admitted from No2 Veterinary Hospital for duty. WM	
	29.4.18		One man transferred to No2 Veterinary Hospital for further training. WM	
	29.4.18		One man reported his arrival from No14 Veterinary Hospital for duty. WM	
	29.4.18		Six sick animals evacuated to IV Corps Veterinary Evacuation Station. WM	
	30.4.18		Eleven sick animals transferred to IV Corps Veterinary Evacuation Station. WM	

W. Stokes Capt RAVC
O.C. 19th Mobile Veterinary Section

[Stamp: 19th MOBILE VETERINARY SECTION 30/4/18]

WAR DIARY.

For the Month ending May 1918.

O.C. 19th Mobile Veterinary Section.

1-6-18.

Army Form C. 2118.

WAR DIARY
or
INTELLIGENCE SUMMARY.
(Erase heading not required.)

Instructions regarding War Diaries and Intelligence Summaries are contained in F. S. Regs., Part II. and the Staff Manual respectively. Title pages will be prepared in manuscript.

Place	Date	Hour	Summary of Events and Information	Remarks and references to Appendices
BOIS de St PIERRE	1-5-18		Five sick animals evacuated to V Corps Veterinary Evacuation Station. WD	
"	2.5.18		Sixteen sick animals evacuated to V Corps Veterinary Evacuation Station. WD	
"	3.5.18		Nine sick animals evacuated to V Corps Veterinary Evacuation Station. WD	
"	4.5.18		Twenty seven sick animals evacuated to V Corps Veterinary Evacuation Station. WD	
"	5.5.18		Eighteen sick animals evacuated to V Corps Veterinary Evacuation Station. WD	
"	6.5.18		Twenty three sick animals evacuated to V Corps Veterinary Evacuation Station. WD	
"	7.5.18		Six sick animals evacuated to V Corps Veterinary Evacuation Station. WD	
"	8.5.18		Ten sick animals evacuated to V Corps Veterinary Evacuation Station. WD	
"	9.5.18		No 13371 L/S Stephens H. admitted to Field Ambulance. WD	
"	10.5.18		Nine sick animals evacuated to V Corps Veterinary Evacuation Station. WD	
"	11.5.18		Two sick animals evacuated to V Corps Veterinary Evacuation Station. WD	
"	12.5.18		Twenty three sick animals evacuated to V Corps Veterinary Evacuation Station. WD	
"	13.5.18		One man reported for duty arrived from No 12 Veterinary Hospital for duty. WD	
"	14.5.18		Nineteen sick animals evacuated to V Corps Veterinary Evacuation Station. WD	
"	15.5.18		Fourteen sick animals evacuated to V Corps Veterinary Evacuation Station. WD	
"	16.5.18		Seven sick animals evacuated to V Corps Veterinary Evacuation Station. WD	
"	17.5.18		No 9326 L/S Harrison to report for aerial from No 12 Veterinary Hospital for duty. WD	
"	18.5.18		Fourteen sick animals evacuated to V Corps Veterinary Evacuation Station. WD	
"	19.5.18		One man admitted to Field Ambulance. WD	
"	20.5.18		Twenty eight sick animals evacuated to V Corps Veterinary Evacuation Station. WD	
"	21.5.18		Sixteen sick animals evacuated to V Corps Veterinary Evacuation Station. WD	
"	22.5.18		Two sick animals evacuated to V Corps Veterinary Evacuation Station. WD	
"	23.5.18		Nothing to report. WD	
"	24.5.18		Six sick animals evacuated to V Corps Veterinary Evacuation Station. WD	
"	25.5.18		Eleven sick animals evacuated to V Corps Veterinary Evacuation Station. WD	
"	26.5.18		Seven sick animals evacuated to V Corps Veterinary Evacuation Station. WD	
"	27.5.18		Two sick animals evacuated to V Corps Veterinary Evacuation Station. WD	
"	28.5.18		Seven sick animals evacuated to V Corps Veterinary Evacuation Station. WD	
"	29.5.18		Nothing to report. WD	
"	30.5.18		Six men sent to V Corps Veterinary Evacuation Station, owing to reduction in ESTABLISHMENT, authority D.A.D.V.S. 42nd DIVISION, No 109, of 25.5.18. WD	
"	31.5.18		Nothing to report. WD	
"			Thirty two sick animals evacuated to IV Corps Veterinary Evacuation Station. WD	
"			Fourteen sick animals evacuated to IV Corps Veterinary Evacuation Station. WD	
"			Eleven sick animals evacuated to IV Corps Veterinary Evacuation Station. WD	

O.C. 19th Mobile Veterinary Section

O I/c AVC Base Records
Woolwich

Herewith Duplicate copies of War Diarys
for Months of Mar. Apr. May & June 1918
please.

BP Stiker Captain
OC 19 MVS.

[Stamp: 19th MOBILE VETERINARY SECTION, No. V 34, Date 1-8-18]

Army Form C. 2118.

WAR DIARY
or
INTELLIGENCE SUMMARY.
(Erase heading not required.)

Instructions regarding War Diaries and Intelligence Summaries are contained in F. S. Regs., Part II. and the Staff Manual respectively. Title pages will be prepared in manuscript.

Place	Date	Hour	Summary of Events and Information	Remarks and references to Appendices
Bois de St Pierre	1.5.18		Eight sick animals evacuated to V Corps Veterinary Evacuation Station.	
"	2.5.18		Sixteen sick animals evacuated to V Corps Veterinary Evacuation Station.	
"	3.5.18		Five sick animals evacuated to V Corps Veterinary Evacuation Station.	
"	4.5.18		Twenty Eight sick animals evacuated to V Corps Veterinary Evacuation Station.	
"	5.5.18		Eighteen sick animals evacuated to V Corps Veterinary Evacuation Station.	
"	6.5.18		Ten sick animals evacuated to V Corps Veterinary Evacuation Station.	
"	7.5.18		Six sick animals evacuated to V Corps Veterinary Evacuation Station.	
"	8.5.18		No 13371 R.A. (Riding) H. admitted to Field Ambulance.	
"	9.5.18		Five sick animals evacuated to V Corps Veterinary Evacuation Station.	
"	10.5.18		Two sick animals evacuated to V Corps Veterinary Evacuation Station.	
"	11.5.18		Twelve sick animals evacuated to V Corps Veterinary Evacuation Station.	
"	12.5.18		Nine Mule sick animals evacuated to V Corps Veterinary Evacuation Station.	
"	13.5.18		One Man reported this evening from Mob. Veterinary Hospital for duty.	
"	14.5.18		Twelve sick animals evacuated to V Corps Veterinary Evacuation Station.	
"	15.5.18		Fourteen sick animals evacuated to V Corps Veterinary Evacuation Station.	
"	16.5.18		Seven sick animals evacuated to V Corps Veterinary Evacuation Station.	
"	17.5.18		No 9326 Lys Hussars, G. Hughes has ceased from the Veterinary Hospital for duty.	
"	18.5.18		Fifteen sick animals evacuated to V Corps Veterinary Evacuation Station.	
"	19.5.18		One Horse sent to Field Ambulance I.V.H.	
"	20.5.18		Eighteen sick animals evacuated to V Corps Veterinary Evacuation Station.	
"	21.5.18		Sixteen sick animals evacuated to V Corps Veterinary Evacuation Station.	
"	22.5.18		Nothing to report.	
"	23.5.18		Six sick animals evacuated to V Corps Veterinary Evacuation Station.	
"	24.5.18		Nothing to report.	
"	25.5.18		Seven sick animals evacuated to V Corps Veterinary Evacuation Station.	
"	26.5.18		Four sick animals evacuated to V Corps Veterinary Evacuation Station.	
"	27.5.18		Five sick animals evacuated to V Corps Veterinary Evacuation Station.	
"	28.5.18		Seven sick animals received at V Corps Veterinary Evacuation Station, owing to reduction in establishment, on being D.A.D.V.S. 42nd Division No 109. G. 25.5.18. W.D.	
"	29.5.18		Nothing to report.	
"	30.5.18		Thirty Two sick animals evacuated to IV Corps Veterinary Evacuation Station.	
"	31.5.18		Fifteen sick animals evacuated to IV Corps Veterinary Evacuation Station. Eleven sick animals evacuated to IV Corps Veterinary Evacuation Station.	

[Signature]
O.C. 19th Mobile Veterinary Section

War Diary.

For the month ending June 1918.

O.C. 19th Mobile Veterinary Section.

*19th MOBILE VETERINARY SECTION
No.
Date 30/6/18*

Army Form C. 2118.

WAR DIARY
or
INTELLIGENCE SUMMARY.
(Erase heading not required.)

Instructions regarding War Diaries and Intelligence Summaries are contained in F. S. Regs., Part II. and the Staff Manual respectively. Title pages will be prepared in manuscript.

Place	Date	Hour	Summary of Events and Information	Remarks and references to Appendices
BOIS du ST PIERRE.	1-6-18		Three sick animals evacuated to IVth CORPS VETERINARY EVACUATION STATION. WD	
"	2-6-18		Seven sick animals evacuated to IVth CORPS VETERINARY EVACUATION STATION. WD	
"	3-6-18		Nothing to report. WD	
"	4-6-18		Eleven sick animals evacuated to IVth CORPS VETERINARY EVACUATION STATION. WD	
"	5-6-18		Nothing to report. WD	
"	6-6-18		Eight sick animals evacuated to IVth CORPS VETERINARY EVACUATION STATION. WD	
"	7-6-18	9-30am	SECTION moved to LOUVENCOURT, and took over camp from O.C. NEW ZEALAND MOBILE VETERINARY SECTION. WD	
LOUVENCOURT.		11-45am	Arrived at LOUVENCOURT. WD	
"	8-6-18		Seven sick animals evacuated to IVth CORPS VETERINARY EVACUATION STATION. WD	
"	9-6-18		Nothing to report. WD	
"	10-6-18		Ten sick animals evacuated to IVth CORPS VETERINARY EVACUATION STATION. WD	
"	11-6-18		Nothing to report. WD	
"	12-6-18		Nine sick animals evacuated to IVth CORPS VETERINARY EVACUATION STATION. WD	
"	13-6-18		Fourteen sick animals evacuated to IVth CORPS VETERINARY EVACUATION STATION. WD	
"	14-6-18		Nothing to report. WD	
"	15-6-18		Six sick animals evacuated to IVth CORPS VETERINARY EVACUATION STATION. WD	
"	16-6-18		One STAFF SERGEANT transferred to No.3 VETERINARY HOSPITAL for duty owing to reduction of ESTABLISHMENT. WD Eight sick animals evacuated to IVth CORPS VETERINARY EVACUATION STATION. WD One ARMY SERVICE CORPS DRIVER transferred to 42nd DIVISIONAL TRAIN for duty being surplus to ESTABLISHMENT. WD	
"	17-6-18		Nothing to report. WD	
"	18-6-18		Twenty two sick animals evacuated to IVth CORPS VETERINARY EVACUATION STATION. WD	
"	19-6-18		Twelve sick animals evacuated to IVth CORPS VETERINARY EVACUATION STATION. WD	
"	20-6-18		Nothing to report. WD	
"	21-6-18		Five sick animals evacuated to IVth CORPS VETERINARY EVACUATION STATION. WD	
"	22-6-18		Five sick animals evacuated to IVth CORPS VETERINARY EVACUATION STATION. WD	
"	23-6-18		Seven sick animals evacuated to IVth CORPS VETERINARY EVACUATION STATION. WD	
"	24-6-18		Nothing to report. WD	
"	25-6-18		One sick animal evacuated to IVth CORPS VETERINARY EVACUATION STATION. WD	
"	26-6-18		Fourteen sick animals evacuated to IVth CORPS VETERINARY EVACUATION STATION. WD	
"	27-6-18		Nothing to report. WD	
"	28-6-18		Eight sick animals evacuated to IVth CORPS VETERINARY EVACUATION STATION. WD	
"	29-6-18		Nothing to report. WD	
"	30-6-18		Nineteen sick animals evacuated to IVth CORPS VETERINARY EVACUATION STATION. WD	

W.Allan Captain
O.C. 19th Mobile Veterinary Section

19th MOBILE VETERINARY SECTION
No.
Date 30/6/18

Army Form C. 2118.

WAR DIARY
of
INTELLIGENCE SUMMARY.

(Erase heading not required.)

Instructions regarding War Diaries and Intelligence Summaries are contained in F. S. Regs., Part II. and the Staff Manual respectively. Title pages will be prepared in manuscript.

Place	Date	Hour	Summary of Events and Information	Remarks and references to Appendices
BOIS d. ST PIERRE	1.6.18		Three sick animals evacuated to IV Corps Veterinary Evacuation Station.	
"	2.6.18		Six sick animals evacuated to IV Corps Veterinary Evacuation Station.	
"	3.6.18		Nothing to report.	
"	4.6.18		Three sick animals evacuated to IV Corps Veterinary Evacuation Station.	
"	5.6.18		Nothing to report.	
"	6.6.18		Eight sick animals evacuated to IV Corps Veterinary Evacuation Station.	
"	7.6.18	7.30am	Section moved to Louvencourt, one pack and one cart from O.C. New Zealand Mobile Veterinary Section.	
LOUVENCOURT	"	11.45am	Section arrived at Louvencourt.	
"	8.6.18		Four sick animals evacuated to 21st Corps Veterinary Evacuation Station.	
"	9.6.18		Nothing to report.	
"	10.6.18		Six sick animals evacuated to IV Corps Veterinary Evacuation Station.	
"	11.6.18		Nothing to report.	
"	12.6.18		Three sick animals evacuated to IV Corps Veterinary Evacuation Station.	
"	13.6.18		Four sick animals evacuated to IV Corps Veterinary Evacuation Station.	
"	14.6.18		Two sick animals evacuated to IV Corps Veterinary Evacuation Station.	
"	15.6.18		Nothing to report.	
"	16.6.18		Six sick animals evacuated to IV Corps Veterinary Evacuation Station. One Staff Sergeant Farrier attached to No.3 Veterinary Hospital Rouen, evacuated, alteration of establishment. Five sick animals evacuated to IV Corps Veterinary Evacuation Station. Supplies to establishment. One Army Service Corps Driver transferred to 142 Divisional Train for duty.	
"	17.6.18		Nothing to report.	
"	18.6.18		Two sick animals evacuated to IV Corps Veterinary Evacuation Station.	
"	19.6.18		Total sick animals evacuated to IV Corps Veterinary Evacuation Station.	
"	20.6.18		Nothing to report.	
"	21.6.18		Five sick animals evacuated to IV Corps Veterinary Evacuation Station.	
"	22.6.18		Five sick animals evacuated to IV Corps Veterinary Evacuation Station.	
"	23.6.18		Seven sick animals evacuated to IV Corps Veterinary Evacuation Station.	
"	24.6.18		Nothing to report.	
"	25.6.18		One sick animal evacuated to IV Corps Veterinary Evacuation Station.	
"	26.6.18		Fourteen sick animals evacuated to IV Corps Veterinary Evacuation Station.	
"	27.6.18		Nothing to report.	
"	28.6.18		Eight sick animals evacuated to IV Corps Veterinary Evacuation Station.	
"	29.6.18		Nothing to report.	
"	30.6.18		Three sick animals evacuated to IV Corps Veterinary Evacuation Station.	

O.C. 19th Mobile Veterinary Section

WAR DIARY

For the month ending July 1918

O6 19th Mobile Veterinary Section

O/c A.V.C. Records
Woolwich

19th MOBILE VETERINARY SECTION
No. C20
Date 13/11/18

Herewith War Diary for the month ending July 1918. please.

W.P.S ——— Capt. A.V.C.
O.C. 19th Mobile Vety Section

Army Form C. 2118.

WAR DIARY
or
INTELLIGENCE SUMMARY.
(Erase heading not required.)

Instructions regarding War Diaries and Intelligence Summaries are contained in F. S. Regs., Part II. and the Staff Manual respectively. Title pages will be prepared in manuscript.

19th MOBILE VETERINARY SECTION
No.
Date 31/7/18

W.R.White Captain
O.C. 19th Mobile Veterinary Section

Place	Date	Hour	Summary of Events and Information	Remarks and references to Appendices
LOUVENCOURT	1-7-18		Eleven sick animals evacuated to No.4 VETERINARY EVACUATION STATION. WRW	
	2-7-18		Seven sick animals evacuated to No.4 VETERINARY EVACUATION STATION. WRW	
	3-7-18		Four sick animals evacuated to No.4 VETERINARY EVACUATION STATION. WRW	
	4-7-18		Six sick animals evacuated to No.4 VETERINARY EVACUATION STATION. WRW	
	5-7-18		Five sick animals evacuated to No.4 VETERINARY EVACUATION STATION. WRW	
	6-7-18		Nothing to report. WRW	
	7-7-18		Twenty two sick animals evacuated to No.4 VETERINARY EVACUATION STATION. WRW	
	8-7-18		Two men admitted to FIELD AMBULANCE. WRW	
			Seven sick animals evacuated to No.4 VETERINARY EVACUATION STATION. WRW	
	9-7-18		One man admitted to FIELD AMBULANCE. WRW	
	10-7-18		Twelve sick animals evacuated to No.4 VETERINARY EVACUATION STATION. WRW	
	11-7-18		Eleven sick animals evacuated to No.4 VETERINARY EVACUATION STATION. WRW	
	12-7-18		Eight sick animals evacuated to No.4 VETERINARY EVACUATION STATION. WRW	
	13-7-18		Thirteen sick animals evacuated to No.4 VETERINARY EVACUATION STATION. WRW	
	14-7-18		Nothing to report. WRW	
	15-7-18		Nothing to report. WRW	
	16-7-18		One man discharged from CASUALTY CLEARING STATION. WRW	
			Nine sick animals evacuated to No.4 VETERINARY EVACUATION STATION. WRW	
	17-7-18		Nothing to report. WRW	
	18-7-18		One sick animal evacuated to No.4 VETERINARY EVACUATION STATION. WRW	
	19-7-18		Seven sick animals evacuated to No.4 VETERINARY EVACUATION STATION. WRW	
	20-7-18		Three men report their arrival from No.4 VETERINARY HOSPITAL for duty. WRW	
	21-7-18		Four sick animals evacuated to No.4 VETERINARY EVACUATION STATION. WRW	
	22-7-18		Nothing to report. WRW	
	23-7-18		Seven sick animals evacuated to No.4 VETERINARY EVACUATION STATION. WRW	
	24-7-18		Nothing to report. WRW	
	25-7-18		Nothing to report. WRW	
	26-7-18		Nine sick animals evacuated to No.4 VETERINARY EVACUATION STATION. WRW	
	27-7-18		Nothing to report. WRW	
	28-7-18		Four sick animals evacuated to No.4 VETERINARY EVACUATION STATION. WRW	
	29-7-18		Nothing to report.	
	30-7-18		Six sick animals evacuated to No.4 VETERINARY HOSPITAL for duty being surplus to establishment. WRW	
			One man sent to No.2 VETERINARY HOSPITAL for duty being surplus to establishment. WRW	
	31-7-18		One sick horse evacuated to No.IV VETERINARY EVACUATION STATION	

Army Form C.

WAR DIARY
or
INTELLIGENCE SUMMARY.

(Erase heading not required.)

Instructions regarding War Diaries and Intelligence Summaries are contained in F. S. Regs., Part II. and the Staff Manual respectively. Title pages will be prepared in manuscript.

Place	Date	Hour	Summary of Events and Information	Remarks and references to Appendices
LOUVENCOURT	1-7-18		Evacuated sick animals to N°4 VETERINARY EVACUATION STATION. L/RS	
	2-7-18		Seven sick animals evacuated to N°4 VETERINARY EVACUATION STATION. L/RS	
	3-7-18		Nine sick animals evacuated to N°4 VETERINARY EVACUATION STATION. L/RS	
	4-7-18		Six sick animals evacuated to N°4 VETERINARY EVACUATION STATION. L/RS	
	5-7-18		Five sick animals evacuated to N°4 VETERINARY EVACUATION STATION. L/RS	
	6-7-18		Nothing to report. L/RS	
	7-7-18		Twenty two sick animals evacuated to N°4 VETERINARY EVACUATION STATION. L/RS	
	8-7-18		Two men admitted to FIELD AMBULANCE. L/RS	
			Seven sick animals evacuated to N°4 VETERINARY EVACUATION STATION. L/RS	
	9-7-18		One man admitted to FIELD AMBULANCE. L/RS	
	10-7-18		Twelve sick animals evacuated to N°4 VETERINARY EVACUATION STATION. L/RS	
	11-7-18		Eleven sick animals evacuated to N°4 VETERINARY EVACUATION STATION. L/RS	
	12-7-18		Eight sick animals evacuated to N°4 VETERINARY EVACUATION STATION. L/RS	
	13-7-18		Fifteen sick animals evacuated to N°4 VETERINARY EVACUATION STATION. L/RS	
	14-7-18		Nothing to report. L/RS	
	15-7-18		Nothing to report. L/RS	
	16-7-18		One man discharged from CASUALTY CLEARING STATION. L/RS	
	17-7-18		Nine sick animals evacuated to N°4 VETERINARY EVACUATION STATION. L/RS	
	18-7-18		Nothing to report. L/RS	
	19-7-18		Six sick animals evacuated to N°4 VETERINARY EVACUATION STATION. L/RS	
			Seven sick animals evacuated to N°4 VETERINARY EVACUATION STATION. L/RS	
	20-7-18		One man report sick & casual from N°4 VETERINARY HOSPITAL for duty. L/RS	
	21-7-18		Four sick animals evacuated to N°4 VETERINARY EVACUATION STATION. L/RS	
	22-7-18		Return to report. L/RS	
	23-7-18		Seven sick animals evacuated to N°4 VETERINARY EVACUATION STATION. L/RS	
	24-7-18		Nothing to report. L/RS	
	25-7-18		Nothing to report. L/RS	
	26-7-18		Nine sick animals evacuated to N°4 VETERINARY EVACUATION STATION. L/RS	
	27-7-18		Nothing to report. L/RS	
	28-7-18		Four sick animals evacuated to N°4 VETERINARY EVACUATION STATION. L/RS	
	29-7-18		Nothing to report. L/RS	
	30-7-18		Six sick animals evacuated to N°4 VETERINARY EVACUATION STATION. L/RS	
			One man sent to N°2 VETERINARY HOSPITAL for duty being surplus to establishment L/RS	
	31-7-18		One sick horse evacuated to Unit IV VETERINARY EVACUATION STATION	

19 Mob Vety Sec
Vol 19

WAR DIARY

for the month ending August 1918

of 19th Mobile Veterinary Section

Army Form C. 2118.

WAR DIARY
or
INTELLIGENCE SUMMARY.
(Erase heading not required.)

Instructions regarding War Diaries and Intelligence Summaries are contained in F. S. Regs., Part II. and the Staff Manual respectively. Title pages will be prepared in manuscript.

Place	Date	Hour	Summary of Events and Information	Remarks and references to Appendices
LOUVENCOURT	1-8-18		Ten sick animals evacuated to IV Veterinary Evacuation Station. M.J.L.	
"	2-8-18		One sick animal " " " " " L.P.S.	
"	3-8-18		Four sick animals " " " " " L.P.S.	
"	4-8-18		Nothing to report. L.P.S.	
"	5-8-18		Four sick animals evacuated to IV Veterinary Evacuation Station L.P.S.	
"	6-8-18		Six " " " " " " L.P.S.	
"	7-8-18		Nothing to report. L.P.S.	
"	8-8-18		Six sick animals evacuated to V Veterinary Evacuation Station L.P.S.	
"	9-8-18		Nothing to report. L.P.S.	
"	10-8-18		Six sick animals evacuated to IV Veterinary Evacuation Station. L.P.S.	
"	11-8-18		Seven sick animals evacuated to II Veterinary Evacuation Station. L.P.S.	
"	12-8-18		Nothing to report. L.P.S.	
"	13-8-18		Six sick animals evacuated to IV Veterinary Evacuation Station. L.P.S.	
"	14-8-18		Nothing to report. L.P.S.	
"	15-8-18		Eight sick animals evacuated to IV Veterinary Evacuation Station. L.P.S.	
"	16-8-18		Six sick animals evacuated to IV Veterinary Evacuation Station. L.P.S.	
"			One category "A" man sent to No.2 Veterinary Hospital for duty. L.P.S.	
"			One man reported his arrival from No.2 Veterinary Hospital. L.P.S.	
"	17-8-18		One sick animal evacuated to IV Veterinary Evacuation Station. L.P.S.	
"	18-8-18		Seven sick animals " " " " " L.P.S.	
"	19-8-18		Nothing to report. L.P.S.	
"	20-8-18		Nothing to report. L.P.S.	
"	21-8-18		Six sick animals evacuated to IV Veterinary Evacuation Station. H.N.L.	
"	22-8-18		Nothing to report. H.N.L.	
"	23-8-18		Nothing to report. H.N.L.	
"	24-8-18		Eight sick animals evacuated to IV Veterinary Evacuation Station. H.N.L.	
"	25-8-18		Nothing to report. H.N.L.	
"			Seven sick animals evacuated to IV Veterinary Evacuation Station. H.N.L.	
BERTRANCOURT	26-8-18	9-45am	Section moved to Bertrancourt. H.N.L.	
"		10-45am	Arrived at Bertrancourt. H.N.L.	
"	27-8-18	9am	Four sick animals evacuated to IV Veterinary Evacuation Station. H.N.L.	
COLINCAMPS		10-30am	Section moved to Colincamps.	
"	28-8-18		Arrived at Colincamps.	
"	28-8-18		Nothing to report. H.N.L.	
"	29-8-18		Nothing to report. H.N.L.	
"	30-8-18		Eight sick animals evacuated to V Veterinary Evacuation Station. H.N.L.	
MIRAUMONT		1-15pm	Section moved to Miraumont.	
"	31-8-18	3-30pm	Arrived at Miraumont. H.N.L.	
"			One man admitted to Field Ambulance. H.N.L.	

H.N. Lord Captain
H.N. Lord Captain
for O.C. 19th Mobile Veterinary Section

Army Form C. 2118.

WAR DIARY
or
INTELLIGENCE SUMMARY
(Erase heading not required.)

Instructions regarding War Diaries and Intelligence Summaries are contained in F. S. Regs., Part II. and the Staff Manual respectively. Title pages will be prepared in manuscript.

Place	Date	Hour	Summary of Events and Information	Remarks and references to Appendices
LOUVENCOURT	1-8-18		Six sick animals evacuated to IV Veterinary Evacuation Station. WPS	
"	2-8-18		One sick animal " " " "	
"	3-8-18		Four sick animals " " "	
"	4-8-18		Nothing to report. WPS	
"	5-8-18		Four sick animals Evacuated to IV Veterinary Evacuation Station. WPS	
"	6-8-18		Six " " " " " " WPS	
"	7-8-18		Nothing to report. WPS	
"	8-8-18		Six sick animals evacuated to IV Veterinary Evacuation Station. WPS	
"	9-8-18		Nothing to report. One sick animal evacuated to IV Veterinary Evacuation Station. WPS	
"	11-8-18		Eleven sick animals evacuated to IV Veterinary Evacuation Station. WPS	
"	12-8-18		Nothing to report. WPS	
"	13-8-18		" " " WPS	
"	14-8-18		Nothing to report. WPS	
"	15-8-18		Eight sick animals evacuated to IV Veterinary Evacuation Station. WPS	
"	16-8-18		Six animals " " " " " WPS	
"	17-8-18		One sick animal evacuated to IV Veterinary Evacuation Station. WPS	
"	18-8-18		" " " " " " " WPS	
"	19-8-18		Six animals " " " " " WPS	
"	20-8-18		Evacuated sick animals to IV Veterinary Evacuation Station. WPS	
"	21-8-18		Nothing to report. NJL	
"	22-8-18		" " " NJL	
"	23-8-18		Eight sick animals evacuated to IV Veterinary Evacuation Station. NJL	
"	24-8-18		Nothing to report. NJL	
"	25-8-18		Seven sick animals evacuated to IV Veterinary Evacuation Station. NJL	
BERTRANCOURT	26-8-18	9.30am	Section moved to BERTRANCOURT. NJL	
"	"	10.30am	Arrived at BERTRANCOURT. NJL	
"	27-8-18	9am	Seven sick animals evacuated to IV Veterinary Evacuation Station. NJL	
COLINCAMPS	28-8-18	10.30am	Section moved to COLINCAMPS. NJL	
"	29-8-18		Nothing to report. NJL	
"	30-8-18		" " " NJL	
MIRAUMONT	31-8-18	1.15pm	Four sick animals evacuated to V Veterinary Evacuation Station. NJL	
		3.30pm	Section moved to MIRAUMONT. NJL	
			Arrived at MIRAUMONT.	
			One horse on Veterinary (Mange) Travelling D.D.S.V.Arr. Monins Crib 8/-. NJL	

WAR DIARY

For the month ending Sept 1918

OC 19th Mobile Veterinary Section

Officer i/c R.A.V.C. Records,
Woolwich Common.

(Dup Copy)

Herewith A.F.C. 2118. for the month ending September 1918. please.

[signature]
Capt. R.A.V.C
O.C. 19th Mobile Vety Section

Army Form C. 2118.

WAR DIARY
or
INTELLIGENCE SUMMARY.
(Erase heading not required.)

Instructions regarding War Diaries and Intelligence Summaries are contained in F. S. Regs., Part II. and the Staff Manual respectively. Title pages will be prepared in manuscript.

Place	Date	Hour	Summary of Events and Information	Remarks and references to Appendices
M.IRAUMONT.	1-9-18		Seven sick animals evacuated to IV"" Corps Veterinary Evacuation Station. WRS	
"	2-9-18		Eleven sick animals evacuated to IV"" Corps Veterinary Evacuation Station. WRS	
"	3-9-18		Nothing to report. WRS	
"	4-9-18	3 P.M.	Fifteen sick animals evacuated to IV"" Corps Veterinary Evacuation Station. WRS	
		5 P.M.	Section moved to WARLENCOURT – EAUCOURT. WRS	
WARLENCOURT- EAUCOURT.			Section arrived at WARLENCOURT – EAUCOURT. WRS	
"	5-9-18		Nothing to report. WRS	
"	6-9-18		Twenty one sick animals evacuated to IV"" Corps Veterinary Evacuation Station. WRS	
"	7-9-18		Nothing to report. WRS	
"	8-9-18		Nothing to report. WRS	
"	9-9-18		Eleven sick animals evacuated to III"" Corps Veterinary Evacuation Station. WRS	
"	10-9-18		Nothing to report. WRS	
"	11-9-18		Nothing to report. WRS	
"	12-9-18		Fifteen sick animals evacuated to IV"" Corps Veterinary Evacuation Station. WRS	
"	13-9-18		One N.C.O. attached to FIELD AMBULANCE. WRS	
"	14-9-18		Nothing to report. WRS	
"	15-9-18		Seven sick animals evacuated to IV"" Corps Veterinary Evacuation Station. WRS	
"	16-9-18		Five sick animals evacuated to IV"" Corps Veterinary Evacuation Station. WRS	
"	17-9-18		Thirty four sick animals evacuated to IV"" Corps Veterinary Hospital. WRS	
"	18-9-18		One man reported his arrival for duty from No. 2 Veterinary Hospital. WRS	
"	19-9-18		Nothing to report. WRS	
"	20-9-18		Five sick animals evacuated to IV"" Corps Veterinary Evacuation Station. WRS	
"	21-9-18	10 A.M.	Five sick animals evacuated to IV"" Corps Veterinary Evacuation Station. WRS	
FREMICOURT.		12-15 P.M.	Section moved to FREMICOURT. WRS	
"			Arrived at FREMICOURT. WRS	
"	22-9-18		Eight sick animals evacuated to IV"" Corps Veterinary Evacuation Station. WRS	
"	23-9-18		Twelve sick animals evacuated to IV"" Corps Veterinary Evacuation Station. WRS	
"			Sixteen sick animals evacuated to IV"" Corps Veterinary Evacuation WRS	
"	24-9-18		One N.C.O. reported his arrival from No. 2 Veterinary Hospital for duty. WRS	
"	25-9-18		Fifteen sick animals evacuated to IV"" Corps Veterinary Evacuation Station. WRS	
"	26-9-18		Twenty seven sick animals evacuated to IV"" Corps Veterinary Evacuation Station. WRS	
"	27-9-18		Thirty four sick animals evacuated to IV"" Corps Veterinary Evacuation Station. WRS	
		3-30 P.M.	Seventeen sick animals evacuated to IV"" Corps Veterinary Evacuation Station. WRS	
LEBUCQUIERE		4-30 P.M.	Section moved to LEBUCQUIERE. WRS	
"	28-9-18		Arrived at LEBUCQUIERE. WRS	
"	29-9-18		Seven sick animals evacuated to IV"" Corps Veterinary Evacuation Station. WRS	
"	30-9-18		Seven sick animals evacuated to IV"" Corps Veterinary Evacuation Station. WRS	
			Fifteen sick animals evacuated to IV"" Corps Veterinary Evacuation Station. WRS	
RUYAULCOURT.		3-30 A.M.	Section moved to RUYAULCOURT. WRS	
		5 P.M.	Section arrived at RUYAULCOURT. WRS	

19th MOBILE 1.10.18

O.C. 19th Mobile Veterinary Section

WAR DIARY or INTELLIGENCE SUMMARY

Army Form C. 2118.

(Erase heading not required.)

Instructions regarding War Diaries and Intelligence Summaries are contained in F. S. Regs., Part II. and the Staff Manual respectively. Title pages will be prepared in manuscript.

Place	Date	Hour	Summary of Events and Information	Remarks and references to Appendices
MIRAUMONT	1.9.18		Seven sick animals evacuated to II Corps Veterinary Evacuation Station. WPS	
	2.9.18		Eleven sick animals evacuated to II Corps Veterinary Evacuation Station. WPS	
	3.9.18		Nothing to report. WPS	
	4.9.18	3 p.m.	Eleven sick animals evacuated to V Corps Veterinary Evacuation Station. WPS	
		5 p.m.	Section moved to WARLENCOURT - EAUCOURT. WPS	
WARLENCOURT EAUCOURT	5.9.18		Section arrived at WARLENCOURT - EAUCOURT. WPS	
	6.9.18		Nothing to report. WPS	
	7.9.18		Twenty one sick animals evacuated to IV Corps Veterinary Evacuation Station. WPS	
	8.9.18		Nothing to report. WPS	
	9.9.18		Nothing to report. WPS	
	10.9.18		Eleven sick animals evacuated to IV Corps Veterinary Evacuation Station. WPS	
	11.9.18		Nothing to report. WPS	
	12.9.18		Nothing to report. WPS	
	13.9.18		Ten sick animals evacuated to IV Corps Veterinary Evacuation Station. WPS	
	14.9.18		One NCO and six OR to No 2 Field Ambulance. WPS	
	15.9.18		Nothing to report. WPS	
	16.9.18		Three sick animals evacuated to IV Corps Veterinary Evacuation Station. WPS	
	17.9.18		One NCO returned to IV Corps Veterinary Hospital. WPS	
	18.9.18		One Man reported sick for duty from No 2 Veterinary Hospital. WPS	
	19.9.18		Nothing to report. WPS	
	20.9.18		Ten sick animals evacuated to IV Corps Veterinary Evacuation Station. WPS	
	21.9.18	10 a.m.	Five sick animals evacuated to IV Corps Veterinary Evacuation Station. WPS	
		12.15 p.m.	Section moved to FREMICOURT. WPS	
FREMICOURT			Section arrived at FREMICOURT. WPS	
	22.9.18		Twelve sick animals evacuated to IV Corps Veterinary Evacuation Station. WPS	
	23.9.18		Seven sick animals evacuated to IV Corps Veterinary Evacuation Station. WPS	
			One NCO reported as ceased from No 2 Veterinary Hospital for duty. WPS	
	24.9.18		Fourteen sick animals evacuated to IV Corps Veterinary Evacuation Station. WPS	
	25.9.18		Forty three sick animals evacuated to IV Corps Veterinary Evacuation Station. WPS	
	26.9.18		Fourteen sick animals evacuated to IV Corps Veterinary Evacuation Station. WPS	
	27.9.18	3.30 p.m.	Section moved to LEBUCQUIERE. WPS	
		4.30 p.m.	Section arrived at LEBUCQUIERE. WPS	
LEBUCQUIERE	28.9.18		Seven sick animals evacuated to IV Corps Veterinary Evacuation Station. WPS	
	29.9.18		Eleven sick animals evacuated to IV Corps Veterinary Evacuation Station. WPS	
	30.9.18		Section and ten sick animals moved to RUYAULCOURT. WPS	
RUYAULCOURT			Section arrived at RUYAULCOURT. WPS	

WAR DIARY

For the month ending October 1918

O.C. 19th Mobile Veterinary Section

O/C R.A.V.C. Records
Woolwich Common

Herewith duplicate copy of War Diary for the month of October 1918. please.

[signature] Capt. R.A.V.C.
OC 19th Mobile Veterinary Section

Army Form C. 2118.

WAR DIARY
INTELLIGENCE SUMMARY.
(Erase heading not required.)

Instructions regarding War Diaries and Intelligence Summaries are contained in F. S. Regs., Part II. and the Staff Manual respectively. Title pages will be prepared in manuscript.

Place	Date	Hour	Summary of Events and Information	Remarks and references to Appendices
RUYAULCOURT	1-10-18		Four sick animals evacuated to IV VETERINARY EVACUATION STATION. WM	
	2-10-18		Fourteen sick animals evacuated to IV VETERINARY EVACUATION STATION WM	
			One man reported his arrival from No 2 VETERINARY HOSPITAL for duty. WM	
"	3-10-18		Seventeen Sick animals evacuated to IV VETERINARY EVACUATION STATION. WM	
"	4-10-18		Fourteen sick animals evacuated to IV VETERINARY EVACUATION STATION WM	
			One man sent to No 2 VETERINARY HOSPITAL for bullet training for A.V.C. SERGEANT to FIELD UNIT. WM	
"	5-10-18		Four sick animals evacuated to IV VETERINARY EVACUATION STATION. WM	
"	6-10-18		Thirty sick animals evacuated to IV VETERINARY EVACUATION STATION. WM	
"	7-10-18		Six sick animals evacuated to IV VETERINARY EVACUATION STATION WM	
"	8-10-18		Twelve sick animals evacuated to IV VETERINARY EVACUATION STATION WM	
	9-10-18	1.P.M.	Section moved to TRESCAULT. WM	
TRESCAULT		3.P.M.	Section arrived at TRESCAULT. WM	
			One sick animal evacuated to IV VETERINARY EVACUATION STATION WM	
LES RUES des VIGNES	10-10-18	Y.R.M.	Section moved to Les RUES des VIGNES. WM	
		10.30.AM.	Section arrived at LES RUES des VIGNES. WM	
"	11-10-18		Nine sick animals evacuated to IV VETERINARY EVACUATION STATION. WM	
	12-10-18	9.30.AM	Section moved to ESNES WM	
ESNES.		10.30.AM	Section arrived at ESNES. WM	
	13-10-18		Six sick animals evacuated to IV VETERINARY EVACUATION STATION. WM	
	14-10-18	8.30.AM	Section moved to BEAUVOIS. WM	
BEAUVOIS		10.30.AM	Section arrived at BEAUVOIS. WM	
"	15-10-18		Five sick animals evacuated to IV VETERINARY EVACUATION STATION. WM	
"	16-10-18		Ten sick animals evacuated to IV VETERINARY EVACUATION STATION. WM	
"	17-10-18		Nothing to report. WM	
"	18-10-18		Four sick animals evacuated to IV VETERINARY EVACUATION STATION. WM	
"	19-10-18		Nothing to report. WM	
"	20-10-18		Three sick animals evacuated to IV VETERINARY EVACUATION STATION. WM	
"	21-10-18		Five sick animals evacuated to IV VETERINARY EVACUATION STATION. WM	
"	22-10-18		Four sick animals evacuated to IV VETERINARY EVACUATION STATION. WM	
"	23-10-18		Five sick animals evacuated to IV VETERINARY EVACUATION STATION. WM	
"	24-10-18		Ten sick animals evacuated to IV VETERINARY EVACUATION STATION. WM	
"	25-10-18		Eleven sick animals evacuated to IV VETERINARY EVACUATION STATION. WM	
"	26-10-18		Nothing to report. WM	
"	27-10-18		Eight sick animals evacuated to V VETERINARY EVACUATION STATION WM	
"	28-10-18		Nothing to report. WM	
"	29-10-18		Four sick animals evacuated to V VETERINARY EVACUATION STATION. WM	
"	30-10-18		Nothing to report. WM	
"	31-10-18		Nothing to report. WM	

O.C. 19th Mobile Veterinary Section

Duplicate Copy of

War Diary

For the month ending October 1918

OC 19th Mobile Veterinary Section.

Army Form C. 2118.

WAR DIARY
INTELLIGENCE SUMMARY

(Erase heading not required.)

Instructions regarding War Diaries and Intelligence Summaries are contained in F. S. Regs., Part II. and the Staff Manual respectively. Title pages will be prepared in manuscript.

Place	Date	Hour	Summary of Events and Information	Remarks and references to Appendices
RUYAULCOURT	1·10·18		Four sick animals evacuated to IV Veterinary Evacuation Station. WDA	
	2·10·18		Fourteen sick animals evacuated to IV Veterinary Evacuation Station WDA	
	3·10·18		One man reported from No 2 Veterinary Hospital for duty.	
	4·10·18		Seventeen sick animals evacuated to IV Veterinary Evacuation Station. WDA	
	5·10·18		Fourteen sick animals evacuated to IV Veterinary Evacuation Station WDA	
			One man sent to No 2 Veterinary Hospital for futher [sic] opinion for A/G. Sergeant to Field Unit. WDA	
	6·10·18		Four sick animals evacuated to IV Veterinary Evacuation Station. WDA	
	7·10·18		Thirty sick animals evacuated to IV Veterinary Evacuation Station WDA	
	8·10·18		Six sick animals evacuated to IV Veterinary Evacuation Station WDA	
	9·10·18		Twelve sick animals evacuated to IV Veterinary Evacuation Station WDA	
TRESCAULT		1.PM	Section moved to TRESCAULT WDA	
		3 PM	Section arrived at TRESCAULT WDA	
	10·10·18		One sick animal evacuated to IV Veterinary Evacuation Station WDA	
LES RUES DES VIGNES		Y P.M	Section moved to LES RUES DES VIGNES WDA	
		10.30 PM	Section arrived at LES RUES DES VIGNES. WDA	
	11·10·18		Nine sick animals evacuated to IV Veterinary Evacuation Station WDA	
ESNES	12·10·18	9.30 AM	Section moved to ESNES WDA	
		10.30 AM	Section arrived at ESNES WDA	
	13·10·18		Six sick animals evacuated to IV Veterinary Evacuation Station WDA	
BEAUVOIS	14·10·18	8.30 AM	Section moved to BEAUVOIS WDA	
		10.30 AM	Section arrived at BEAUVOIS WDA	
	15·10·18		Four sick animals evacuated to IV Veterinary Evacuation Station WDA	
"	16·10·18		Ten sick animals evacuated to IV Veterinary Evacuation Station WDA	
"	17·10·18		Nothing to report WDA	
"	18·10·18		Four sick animals evacuated to IV Veterinary Evacuation Station. WDA	
"	19·10·18		Nothing to report WDA	
"	20·10·18		Four sick animals evacuated to IV Veterinary Evacuation Station. WDA	
"	21·10·18		Five sick animals evacuated to IV Veterinary Evacuation Station. WDA	
"	22·10·18		Four sick animals evacuated to IV Veterinary Evacuation Station. WDA	
"	23·10·18		Five sick animals evacuated to IV Veterinary Evacuation Station. WDA	
"	24·10·18		Ten sick animals evacuated to IV Veterinary Evacuation Station. WDA	
"	25·10·18		Eleven sick animals evacuated to IV Veterinary Evacuation Station. WDA	
"	26·10·18		Nothing to report. WDA	
"	27·10·18		Nine sick animals evacuated to V Veterinary Evacuation Station WDA	
"	28·10·18		Nothing to report. WDA	
"	29·10·18		Four sick animals evacuated to IV Veterinary Evacuation Station WDA	
"	30·10·18		Nothing to report. WDA	
"	31·10·18		Nothing to report. WDA	

OC 19th Mobile Veterinary Section

War Diary

For the month ending November 1918.

O.C. 19th Mobile Veterinary Section

Army Form C. 2118.

WAR DIARY
or
INTELLIGENCE SUMMARY.
(Erase heading not required.)

Instructions regarding War Diaries and Intelligence Summaries are contained in F. S. Regs., Part II. and the Staff Manual respectively. Title pages will be prepared in manuscript.

Place	Date	Hour	Summary of Events and Information	Remarks and references to Appendices
BEAUVOIS.	1-11-18		Two sick animals evacuated to IV Veterinary Evacuation Station. LPP	
"	2-11-18		Nothing to report. LPP	
"	3-11-18		Four sick animals evacuated to IV Veterinary Evacuation Station. LPP	
"	4-11-18	11.45am	Section moved to SOLESMES. LPP	
SOLESMES		3 pm	Section arrived at SOLESMES. LPP	
"	5-11-18		Three sick animals evacuated to IV Veterinary Evacuation Station. LPP	
"	6-11-18	11.30am	Section moved to LE QUESNOY. LPP	
LE QUESNOY		4 pm	Section arrived at LE QUESNOY. LPP	
"	7-11-18		Ten sick animals evacuated to IV Veterinary Evacuation Station. LPP	
"	8-11-18		Nine sick animals evacuated to VI Veterinary Evacuation Station. LPP	
"	9-11-18	8.30am	Four sick animals evacuated to HARGNIES. LPP	
HARGNIES		2 pm	Section arrived at HARGNIES. LPP	
"	10-11-18		Six sick animals evacuated to IV Veterinary Evacuation Station. LPP	
"	11-11-18		Nothing to report. LPP	
"	12-11-18		Nothing to report. LPP	
"	13-11-18		Seven sick animals evacuated to IV Veterinary Evacuation Station. LPP	
"	14-11-18		Fourteen sick animals evacuated to IV Veterinary Evacuation Station. LPP	
"	15-11-18		Twenty one sick animals evacuated to IV Veterinary Evacuation Station. LPP	
"	16-11-18		Twenty four sick animals evacuated to IV Veterinary Evacuation Station. LPP	
"	17-11-18		Nothing to report. LPP	
"	18-11-18		Nothing to report. LPP	
"	19-11-18		Nothing to report. LPP	
"	20-11-18		Seventy nine sick animals evacuated to IV Veterinary Evacuation Station. LPP	
"	21-11-18		Nothing to report. LPP	
"	22-11-18		Eight sick animals evacuated to IV Veterinary Evacuation Station. LPP	
"	23-11-18		Eleven sick animals evacuated to IV Veterinary Evacuation Station. LPP	
"	24-11-18		Fourteen sick animals evacuated to IV Veterinary Evacuation Station. LPP	
"	25-11-18		Six sick animals evacuated to IV Veterinary Evacuation Station. LPP	
"	26-11-18		Nothing to report. LPP	
"	27-11-18		Five sick animals evacuated to IV Veterinary Evacuation Station. LPP	
"	28-11-18		Nothing to report. LPP	
"	29-11-18		Nothing to report. LPP	
"	30-11-18		Nothing to report. LPP	

OC 19th Mobile Veterinary Section

Army Form C. 2118

WAR DIARY
or
INTELLIGENCE SUMMARY.
(Erase heading not required.)

Instructions regarding War Diaries and Intelligence Summaries are contained in F. S. Regs., Part II. and the Staff Manual respectively. Title pages will be prepared in manuscript.

Place	Date	Hour	Summary of Events and Information	Remarks and references to Appendices
BEAUVOIS	1.11.18		Two sick animals evacuated to 19th Veterinary Evacuation Station. LM	
"	2.11.18		Nothing to report. LM	
"	3.11.18		Sick animals evacuated to 19th Veterinary Evacuation Station. LM	
"	4.11.18	11.45am	Section moved to SOLESMES. LM	
SOLESMES	"	3 pm	Section arrived at SOLESMES. LM	
"	5.11.18		Sick animals evacuated to 19th Veterinary Evacuation Station. LM	
"	6.11.18	11.30am	Section moved to LE QUESNOY. LM	
LE QUESNOY	"	4 pm	Section arrived at LE QUESNOY. LM	
"	7.11.18		Sick animals evacuated to 19th Veterinary Evacuation Station. LM	
"	8.11.18		Sick animals evacuated to 19th Veterinary Evacuation Station. LM	
"	9.11.18		Sick animals evacuated to HARGNIES. LM	
HARGNIES	"	8.30am	Section moved to HARGNIES. LM	
"	"	2 pm	Section arrived at HARGNIES. LM	
"	10.11.18		Nothing to report. LM	
"	11.11.18		Sick animals evacuated to 19th Veterinary Evacuation Station. LM	
"	12.11.18		Nothing to report. LM	
"	13.11.18		Nothing to report. LM	
"	14.11.18		Sick animals evacuated to 19th Veterinary Evacuation Station. LM	
"	15.11.18		Sick animals evacuated to 19th Veterinary Evacuation Station. LM	
"	16.11.18		Sick animals evacuated to 19th Veterinary Evacuation Station. LM	
"	17.11.18		Sick animals evacuated to 19th Veterinary Evacuation Station. LM	
"	18.11.18		Nothing to report. LM	
"	19.11.18		Nothing to report. LM	
"	20.11.18		Sick animals evacuated to 19th Veterinary Evacuation Station. LM	
"	21.11.18		Nothing to report. LM	
"	22.11.18		Sick animals evacuated to 19th Veterinary Evacuation Station. LM	
"	23.11.18		Sick animals evacuated to 19th Veterinary Evacuation Station. LM	
"	24.11.18		Sick animals evacuated to 19th Veterinary Evacuation Station. LM	
"	25.11.18		Nothing to report. LM	
"	26.11.18		Nothing to report. LM	
"	27.11.18		Sick animals evacuated to 19th Veterinary Evacuation Station. LM	
"	28.11.18		Nothing to report. LM	
"	29.11.18		Nothing to report. LM	
"	30.11.18		Nothing to report. LM	

WAR DIARY.

For the month ending December 1918.

O.C. 19th Mobile Veterinary Section.

Officer Commanding
No. 19 M.V.S.

[Stamp: OFFICER-IN-CHARGE RECORDS No. 3/1864/19 26 APR 1919 ROYAL ARMY VETY. CORPS.]

Re/ reverse

I beg to acknowledge receipt of war diaries dated from:—
1-12-18 to 31-3-19.

N.A.Bates
Capt for Lt Col
i/c Records R.A.V.C.

[Stamp: OFFICER-IN-CHARGE RECORDS 6-MAY 1919 ROYAL ARMY VETY. CORPS.]

Woolwich
23-4-19

O i/c RAVC Records
Woolwich

As the Cadre of the above Unit is about to
go to UK. Herewith duplicate copies
of AF C 2118 to date.

Kindly acknowledge receipt.

W P Stoker Capt RAVC
oc 19 MVS

Stamp: NO. 19 MOBILE VETERINARY SECTION — Date 31/3/19

Stamp: OFFICER-IN-CHARGE RECORDS — 16 APR 1919 — ROYAL ARMY VETY. CORPS.

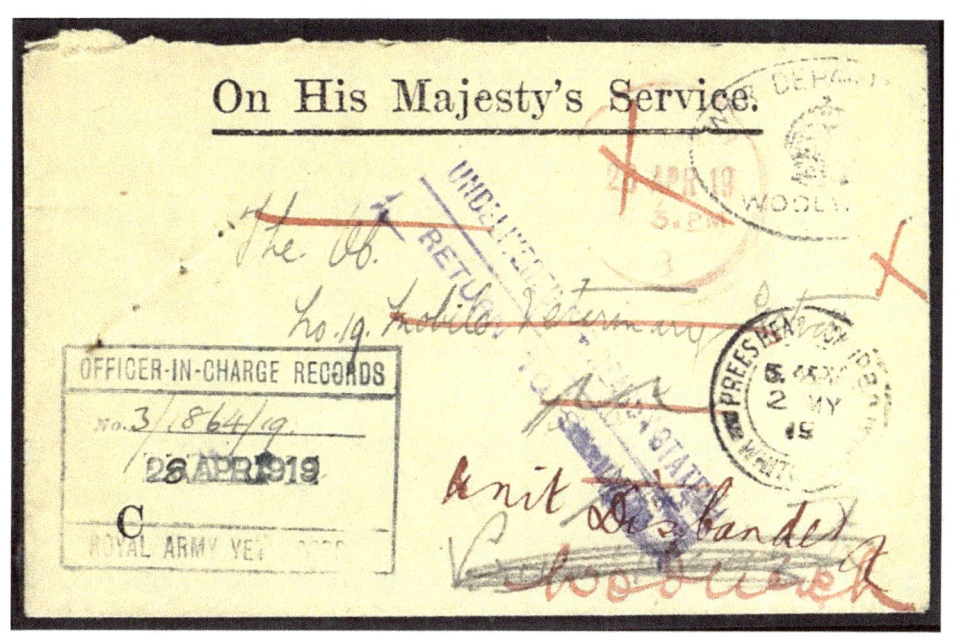

Army Form C. 2118.

WAR DIARY
or
INTELLIGENCE SUMMARY.
(Erase heading not required.)

Instructions regarding War Diaries and Intelligence Summaries are contained in F. S. Regs. Part II. and the Staff Manual respectively. Title pages will be prepared in manuscript.

Place	Date	Hour	Summary of Events and Information	Remarks and references to Appendices
HARGNIES.	1-12-18		Four sick animals evacuated to IV Veterinary Evacuation Station. WPS	
	2-12-18		Nothing to report. WPS	
	3-12-18		Nothing to report. WPS	
	4-12-18		Ten sick animals evacuated to IV Veterinary Evacuation Station. WPS.	
	5-12-18		Nothing to report. WPS	
	6-12-18		Section sick animals evacuated to IV Veterinary Evacuation Station. WPS	
	7-12-18		Nothing to report. WPS	
	8-12-18		Nine sick animals evacuated to IV Veterinary Evacuation Station. WPS	
	9-12-18		Nothing to report. WPS	
	10-12-18		Nothing to report. WPS	
	11-12-18		Ten sick animals evacuated to IV Veterinary Evacuation Station. WPS	
	12-12-18		Nothing to report. WPS	
	13-12-18		Nothing to report. WPS	
	14-12-18	10.30 a.m.	Section moved to MARPENT. WPS	
MARPENT		4 p.m.	Section arrived at MORPENT. WPS	
	15-12-18	10 a.m.	Section moved to LOBBES. WPS	
LOBBES.		2.30 p.m.	Section arrived at LOBBES. WPS	
	16-12-18		Twenty four sick animals evacuated to IV Veterinary Evacuation Station. WPS	
	17-12-18		Nothing to report. WPS	
	18-12-18	10.30 a.m.	Section moved to GILLY. WPS	
GILLY		4 p.m.	Section arrived at GILLY. WPS	
	19-12-18		Ten sick animals evacuated to IV Veterinary Evacuation Station. WPS	
	20-12-18		Nothing to report. WPS	
	21-12-18		Nothing to report. WPS	
	22-12-18		Twelve sick animals evacuated to IV Veterinary Evacuation Station. WPS	
	23-12-18		Nine sick animals evacuated to IV Veterinary Evacuation Station. WPS	
	24-12-18		Nothing to report. WPS	
	25-12-18		Forty four sick animals evacuated to IV Veterinary Evacuation Station. WPS	
	26-12-18		Nothing to report. WPS	
	27-12-18		Nothing to report. WPS	
	28-12-18		Nothing to report. WPS	
	29-12-18		Nothing to report. WPS	
	30-12-18		Nothing to report. WPS	
	31-12-18		Ten sick animals evacuated to IV Veterinary Evacuation Station. WPS	

W. Otton, Capt. RAVC
O.C. 19th Mobile Veterinary Section

19th MOBILE VETERINARY SECTION
No. Date 31/12/18

Army Form C. 2118.

OFFICER-IN-CHARGE RECORDS
16 APR 1919
ROYAL ARMY VETY. CORPS.

WAR DIARY
or
INTELLIGENCE SUMMARY.
(Erase heading not required.)

Instructions regarding War Diaries and Intelligence Summaries are contained in F. S. Regs., Part II. and the Staff Manual respectively. Title pages will be prepared in manuscript.

Place	Date	Hour	Summary of Events and Information	Remarks and references to Appendices
MARGNES	1.12.18		Four sick animals evacuated to 10th Veterinary Evacuation Station. LM	
"	2.12.18		Nothing to report. WD	
"	3.12.18		Nothing to report. WD	
"	4.12.18		One sick animal evacuated to 10th Veterinary Evacuation Station. WS	
"	5.12.18		Nothing to report. WM	
"	6.12.18		British sick animals evacuated to 10th Veterinary Evacuation Station. WM	
"	7.12.18		Nothing to report. WM	
"	8.12.18		Four sick animals evacuated to 10th Veterinary Evacuation Station. WM	
"	9.12.18		Nothing to report. WM	
"	10.12.18		Nothing to report. WM	
"	11.12.18		Six sick animals evacuated to 10th Veterinary Evacuation Station. WM	
"	12.12.18		Nothing to report. WM	
"	13.12.18		Nothing to report. WM	
"	14.12.18	10-30am	Section moved to MORPENT. WS	
MORPENT	"	4 pm	Section arrived at MORPENT. WM	
"	15.12.18	10 am	Section moved to LOBBES. WM	
LOBBES	"	2.30 pm	Section arrived at LOBBES. WM	
"	16.12.18		Twenty four sick animals evacuated to 19th Veterinary Evacuation Station. WM	
"	17.12.18		Nothing to report. WM	
"	18.12.18	10-30 am	Section moved to GILLY. WM	
GILLY	"	4 pm	Section arrived at GILLY. WM	
"	19.12.18		Six sick animals evacuated to 19th Veterinary Evacuation Station. WM	
"	20.12.18		Nothing to report. WM	
"	21.12.18		Several sick animals evacuated to 19th Veterinary Evacuation Station. WM	
"	22.12.18		Five sick animals evacuated to 19th Veterinary Evacuation Station. WM	
"	23.12.18		Nothing to report. WM	
"	24.12.18		Fifty four sick animals evacuated to 19th Veterinary Evacuation Station. WM	
"	25.12.18		Nothing to report. WM	
"	26.12.18		Nothing to report. WM	
"	27.12.18		Nothing to report. WM	
"	28.12.18		Nothing to report. WM	
"	29.12.18		Nothing to report. WM	
"	30.12.18		Nothing to report. WM	
"	31.12.18		Six sick animals evacuated to 19th Veterinary Evacuation Station. WM	

NO. 19 MOBILE VETERINARY SECTION
31/12/18

W. Whelan Capt. R.A.V.C.
O.C. 19th Mobile Veterinary Section

WAR DIARY.

For the Month ending January 1919.

O.C. 19th Mobile Veterinary Section.

WAR DIARY
or
INTELLIGENCE SUMMARY.
(Erase heading not required.)

Army Form C. 2118.

Instructions regarding War Diaries and Intelligence Summaries are contained in F. S. Regs., Part II. and the Staff Manual respectively. Title pages will be prepared in manuscript.

Place	Date	Hour	Summary of Events and Information	Remarks and references to Appendices
GILLY	1-1-19		Eight sick animals evacuated to IVth VETERINARY EVACUATION STATION. WD	
	2-1-19		Nothing to report. WD	
	3-1-19		One man admitted to FIELD AMBULANCE. WD	
	4-1-19		Ten sick animals evacuated to IVth VETERINARY EVACUATION STATION. WD	
	5-1-19		Nothing to report. WD	
	6-1-19		Six sick animals evacuated to IVth VETERINARY EVACUATION STATION. WD	
	7-1-19		Nothing to report. WD	
	8-1-19		Nothing to report. WD	
	9-1-19		Nothing to report. WD	
	10-1-19		Nothing to report. WD	
	11-1-19		Six sick animals evacuated to IVth VETERINARY EVACUATION STATION. WD	
	12-1-19		One man discharged from FIELD AMBULANCE. WD	
	13-1-19		Nothing to report. WD	
	14-1-19		Nothing to report. WD	
	15-1-19		Nothing to report. WD	
	16-1-19		Nothing to report. WD	
	17-1-19		Nothing to report. WD	
	18-1-19		One Corporal appointed Paid/Sergeant, authority R.A.V.C. BASE RECORDS, LOCAL CORPS ORDERS. No 7/12/22/19 dated 14-1-19. WD	
	19-1-19		Nothing to report. WD	
	20-1-19		Two sick animals evacuated to ADVANCED VETERINARY HOSPITAL. WD	
	21-1-19		Sixteen animals classified D. evacuated to IVth VETERINARY EVACUATION STATION. WD	
	22-1-19		Nine sick animals evacuated to IVth VETERINARY EVACUATION STATION. WD	
	23-1-19		Nothing to report. WD	
	24-1-19		Nothing to report. WD	
	25-1-19		Nothing to report. WD	
	26-1-19		One sick animal evacuated to ADVANCED VETERINARY HOSPITAL. WD Six animals reclassified C. returned from IVth VETERINARY EVACUATION STATION and distributed to UNITS. WD	
	27-1-19		Nothing to report. WD	
	28-1-19		Nothing to report. WD	
	29-1-19		Nothing to report. WD	
	30-1-19		Six animals reclassified C. returned from IVth VETERINARY EVACUATION STATION and distributed to UNITS. WD	
	31-1-19		Nothing to report. WD	

OC. 19th Mobile Veterinary Section
Capt R.A.V.C.
31/1/19
19th MOBILE VETERINARY SECTION

Army Form C. 2118.

WAR DIARY
or
INTELLIGENCE SUMMARY.
(Erase heading not required.)

Instructions regarding War Diaries and Intelligence Summaries are contained in F. S. Regs., Part II. and the Staff Manual respectively. Title pages will be prepared in manuscript.

Place	Date	Hour	Summary of Events and Information	Remarks and references to Appendices
GILLY	1-1-19		Eight sick animals evacuated to 18th VETERINARY EVACUATION STATION WRS	
	2-1-19		Nothing to report WRS	
	3-1-19		One man admitted to FIELD AMBULANCE WRS	
	4-1-19		Ten sick animals evacuated to 18th VETERINARY EVACUATION STATION, WRS	
	5-1-19		Nothing to report WRS	
	6-1-19		Six sick animals evacuated to 18th VETERINARY EVACUATION STATION WRS	
	7-1-19		Nothing to report WRS	
	8-1-19		Nothing to report WRS	
	9-1-19		Nothing to report WRS	
	10-1-19		Nothing to report WRS	
	11-1-19		Eight sick animals evacuated to 18th VETERINARY EVACUATION STATION WRS	
	12-1-19		One man discharged from FIELD AMBULANCE WRS	
	13-1-19		Nothing to report WRS	
	14-1-19		Nothing to report WRS	
	15-1-19		Nothing to report WRS	
	16-1-19		Nothing to report WRS	
	17-1-19		Nothing to report WRS	
	18-1-19		Sergeant R. Ricketts Pte/Sergeant, authority R.A.V.C. BASE RECORDS, LOCAL CORPS ORDERS No 7469/2/19 dated 14-1-19.	
	19-1-19		Nothing to report WRS	
	20-1-19		Two sick animals evacuated to ADVANCED VETERINARY HOSPITAL WRS	
	21-1-19		Ordinary classifact 3 evacuated to 18th VETERINARY EVACUATION STATION WRS	
	22-1-19		Three SICK animals evacuated to 18th VETERINARY EVACUATION STATION WRS	
	23-1-19		Nothing to report WRS	
	24-1-19		Nothing to report WRS	
	25-1-19		Nothing to report WRS	
	26-1-19		Two sick animals evacuated to ADVANCED VETERINARY HOSPITAL WRS	
	27-1-19		One animal declared Cast C returned from 18th VETERINARY EVACUATION STATION	
	28-1-19		Nothing to report WRS	
	29-1-19		Two Casts C pastaurifred C returned from 18th VETERINARY EVACUATION STATION and distributed to UNITS WRS	
	30-1-19		Nothing to report WRS	
	31-1-19		Nothing to report WRS	

R Roker Capt R.A.V.C.
O.C. 18th Mobile Veterinary Section

WAR DIARY
19th M.V.S. 42nd
February 1919

WAR DIARY
or
INTELLIGENCE SUMMARY

Army Form C. 2118.

Place	Date	Hour	Summary of Events and Information	Remarks and references to Appendices
Gilly	1/2/19		Nothing to report WD	
"	2/2/19		Nothing to report WD	
"	3/2/19		Nothing to report WD	
"	4/2/19		Nothing to report WD	
"	5/2/19		Nothing to report WD	
"	6/2/19		Nothing to report WD	
"	7/2/19		One sick animal evacuated to ADVANCED VETERINARY HOSPITAL WD.	
"	8/2/19		Nothing to report WD	
"	9/2/19		Eight sick animals evacuated to ADVANCED VETERINARY HOSPITAL WD.	
"	10/2/19		Eighty four sick animals evacuated to No. FOUR VETERINARY EVACUATION STATION WD.	
"	11/2/19		Four sick animals evacuated to ADVANCED VETERINARY HOSPITAL WD	
"	12/2/19		Nothing to report WD	
"	13/2/19		Nine sick animals evacuated to ADVANCED VETERINARY HOSPITAL WD	
"	14/2/19		Nothing to report WD	
"	15/2/19		Nothing to report WD	
"	16/2/19		One sick animal evacuated to ADVANCED VETERINARY HOSPITAL WD	
"	17/2/19		Nothing to report WD	
"	18/2/19		Nothing to report WD	
"	19/2/19		Nothing to report WD	
"	20/2/19		One man discharged from hospital WD	
"	21/2/19		Nothing to report WD	
"	22/2/19		Nothing to report WD	
"	23/2/19		One NCO admitted to FIELD AMBULANCE WD	
"	24/2/19		One man admitted to FIELD AMBULANCE WD	
"	25/2/19		Nothing to report WD	
"	26/2/19		Nothing to report WD	
"	27/2/19		One NCO admitted to FIELD AMBULANCE WD	
"	28/2/19		Nothing to report WD	

Capt RAVC
o/c 191 Mobile Vet Section

Army Form C. 2118.

WAR DIARY
or
INTELLIGENCE SUMMARY.
(Erase heading not required.)

Instructions regarding War Diaries and Intelligence Summaries are contained in F. S. Regs., Part II. and the Staff Manual respectively. Title pages will be prepared in manuscript.

28.2.19

Place	Date	Hour	Summary of Events and Information	Remarks and references to Appendices
Gully	1/2/19		Nothing to report APM	
"	2/2/19		Nothing to report APM	
"	3/2/19		Nothing to report APM	
"	4/2/19		Nothing to report APM	
"	5/2/19		Nothing to report APM	
"	6/2/19		Nothing to report APM	
"	7/2/19		One sick animal evacuated to ADVANCED VETERINARY HOSPITAL APM	
"	8/2/19		Nothing to report APM	
"	9/2/19		Eight sick animals evacuated to ADVANCED VETERINARY HOSPITAL APM	
"	10/2/19		Eighty four sick animals evacuated to No FOUR VETERINARY EVACUATION STATION	
"	11/2/19		Four sick animals evacuated to ADVANCED VETERINARY HOSPITAL APM	
"	12/2/19		Nothing to report APM	
"	13/2/19		Nine sick animals evacuated to ADVANCED VETERINARY HOSPITAL APM	
"	14/2/19		Nothing to report APM	
"	15/2/19		Nothing to report APM	
"	16/2/19		One sick animal evacuated to ADVANCED VETERINARY HOSPITAL APM	
"	17/2/19		Nothing to report APM	
"	18/2/19		Nothing to report APM	
"	19/2/19		Nothing to report APM	
"	20/2/19		One extra clothing store required APM	
"	21/2/19		Nothing to report APM	
"	22/2/19		Nothing to report APM	
"	23/2/19		One NCO admitted to FIELD AMBULANCE APM	
"	24/2/19		One man admitted to FIELD AMBULANCE APM	
"	25/2/19		Nothing to report APM	
"	26/2/19		Nothing to report APM	
"	27/2/19		One NCO admitted to FIELD AMBULANCE APM	
"	28/2/19		Nothing to report APM	

Capt RAVC
O/C Mobile Sec

Vol 27

War Diary.

19th Mobile Vety Sec.

From 1/3/19 to 31/3/19

19

42 DIV

Army Form C. 2118.

WAR DIARY
or
INTELLIGENCE SUMMARY.
(Erase heading not required.)

Instructions regarding War Diaries and Intelligence Summaries are contained in F. S. Regs., Part II. and the Staff Manual respectively. Title pages will be prepared in manuscript.

Place	Date	Hour	Summary of Events and Information	Remarks and references to Appendices
Gilly	1/3/19		Sale of 7 Animals. Obtained CHARLEROI. WRS	
"	2/3/19		Nothing to report. WRS	
"	3/3/19		Nothing to report. WRS	
"	4/3/19		Sale of 7 Animals at CHARLEROI. WRS	
"	5/3/19		Nothing to report. WRS	
"	6/3/19		Nothing to report. WRS	
"	7/3/19		Sale of 2 Animals at CHARLEROI. WRS	
"	8/3/19		Sale of 2 Animals at CHARLEROI. WRS	
"	9/3/19		Nothing to Report. WRS	
"	10/3/19		Nothing to report. WRS	
"	11/3/19		Sale of 7 Animals at CHARLEROI. WRS	
"	12/3/19		Nothing to report. WRS	
"	13/3/19		Sale of 12 Animals at CHARLEROI. WRS	
"	14/3/19		Nothing to report. WRS	
"	15/3/19		Nothing to report. WRS	
"	16/3/19		Nothing to report. WRS	
"	17/3/19		Nothing to report. WRS	
"	18/3/19		Nothing to report. WRS	
"	19/3/19		Handed over equipment of the Section to O.C. No 1 Coy. No 2 Div. Train & also obtainment of deficiencies WRS	
"	20/3/19		Nothing to report. WRS	
"	21/3/19		Eighteen men transferred to No.4 V.E.S. WRS	
"	22/3/19		Nine men reported arrival from No.4 V.E.S. to form the Cadre WRS	
"	23/3/19		One Sgt. reported his arrival from 93rd Bde. A.F.A. to take charge of the Cadre WRS	
"	24/3/19		Nothing to report. WRS	
"	25/3/19		G.1098 Eq. DEMOBILISATION COPY completed, signed according to demobilisation instructions and all Indents for Deficiencies Submitted. WRS	
"	26/3/19		Nothing to report. WRS	
"	27/3/19		Nothing to report. WRS	
"	28/3/19		Nothing to report. WRS	
"	29/3/19		Nothing to report. WRS	
"	30/3/19		Nothing to report. WRS	
"	31/3/19		Nothing to report. WRS	

WPStephen Capt AVC
oc 19th Mob Vety Section

Army Form C. 2118.

WAR DIARY
or
INTELLIGENCE SUMMARY.
(Erase heading not required.)

Instructions regarding War Diaries and Intelligence Summaries are contained in F. S. Regs., Part II. and the Staff Manual respectively. Title pages will be prepared in manuscript.

Place	Date	Hour	Summary of Events and Information	Remarks and references to Appendices
Gilly	1/3/19		Sale of 7 Animals conducted CHARLEROI 10PM	
	2/3/19		Nothing to report 10PM	
	3/3/19		Nothing to report 10PM	
	4/3/19		Sale of 7 Animals at CHARLEROI 10PM	
	5/3/19		Nothing to report 10PM	
	6/3/19		Nothing to report 10PM	
	7/3/19		Sale of 2 Animals at CHARLEROI 10PM	
	8/3/19		Sale of 7 Animals at CHARLEROI 10PM	
	9/3/19		Nothing to report 10PM	
	10/3/19		Nothing to report 10PM	
	11/3/19		Sale of 2 Animals at CHARLEROI 10PM	
	12/3/19		Nothing to report 10PM	
	13/3/19		Sale of 12 Animals at CHARLEROI 10PM	
	14/3/19		Nothing to report 10PM	
	15/3/19		Nothing to report 10PM	
	16/3/19		Nothing to report 10PM	
	17/3/19		Nothing to report 10PM	
	18/3/19		Nothing to report 10PM	
	19/3/19		Handed over equipment of the Section to I.O.C. N°1 Coy. H.2 Div. Train & also detachment of depôt men 10PM	ac/s
	20/3/19		Nothing to report 10PM	
	21/3/19		English men transferred to N°4 V.E.S. 10PM	
	22/3/19		N°4 V.E.S. to form the Cadre 10PM	
	23/3/19		One man reported return from 93 Bde A.F.A. to take charge of the Cadre 10PM	
	24/3/19		One Sgt. reported to report 10PM	
	25/3/19		Nothing to report 10PM	
	26/3/19		G.1094 & 89 DEMOBILISATION COPY completed signed according to demobilization instructions and all returns	10PM
	27/3/19		Nothing to report 10PM for Deficiencies submitted	
	28/3/19		Nothing to report 10PM	
	29/3/19		Nothing to report 10PM	
	30/3/19		Nothing to report 10PM	
	31/3/19		[illegible]	

W.R.Sinclair Capt AVC
OC 19th Mob Vety Section

www.ingramcontent.com/pod-product-compliance
Lightning Source LLC
Chambersburg PA
CBHW081557160426
43191CB00011B/1959